If I were asked to make a list of the top 1 percent of family experts who know the hearts of teens and can express those needs to their parents, Tim Smith heads my list. If you want to stay close and connected to your busy, emotional, wonderful, challenging teen, Tim's grace-laced, trust-building parenting truths will help you, just like they've helped Cindy and me with our teenagers. In case you haven't heard, your teen is "crying" for you to get this book!

John Trent, Ph.D.
Author of The Light of Home *and President of StrongFamilies.com*

The Seven Cries of Today's Teens alerts parents and youth workers to the reality that teenagers live in a culture that doesn't protect them, that hurries them into adulthood and adult-sized problems without preparing them to handle them. I appreciated the hopeful language that parents can respond to the cries by valuing their teenagers enough not to leave them alone.

Doug Fields
Youth Pastor, Saddleback Community Church (Lake Forest, CA) and Author of Purpose-Driven Youth Ministry

This analysis of today's teens is based not only on the latest research available, but on the careful observation and hands-on experience of one of America's top youth ministry professionals. Tim Smith has spent many years listening to the desperate cries of young people who just want to be heard. In this book you will hear their voices, their message to us all.

Wayne Rice
Director of Understanding Your Teenager

Not only is this book solid and es   getting
inside the private life of the Amer   n culture are difficult to read. Tim Smit   urner.
I kept waiting to see what was cc

President of Youthbuilders

It's hard to hear the deep cry of our teenagers' hearts over the background din of their culture. Tim Smith has turned up the volume on those cries loud enough for parents to detect them. For those parents willing to listen, and listen closely, Smith has made it possible for a connection at the heart that every teen longs for with their parents.

Tim Kimmel
Author of Little House on the Freeway

I've been listening to the cries of today's youth culture for over two decades. No doubt, they're getting louder. Tim Smith has helped me and a generation of parents to hear, recognize, and most importantly, respond in a way that will begin to answer and quiet these cries. *The Seven Cries of Today's Teens* isn't just a one-time read. It's a helpful tool you'll come back to again and again.

Walt Mueller
President of The Center for Parent/Youth Understanding

As a youth pastor, I am looking for ways to help parents and youth-workers develop the skills of loving, communicating to, and discipling teenagers. *The Seven Cries of Today's Teens* is a combination of "in the trenches" experience and excellent research that compels anyone who reads it to reshape their thinking about teenagers. This book is an excellent resource with practical application that is invaluable for any parent, teacher, or youthworker.

Michael Katzenberger
*Student Ministries Pastor, Calvary Community Church
(Westlake Village, CA)*

The Seven Cries of Today's Teens

Hear Their Hearts,

Make the Connection

BY TIM SMITH

INTEGRITY®

PUBLISHERS

Nashville

The Seven Cries of Today's Teens

Copyright © 2003 by Tim Smith

Published by Integrity Publishers, a division of Integrity Media, Inc., 5250 Virginia Way, Suite 110, Brentwood, TN 37027.

HELPING PEOPLE WORLDWIDE EXPERIENCE *the* MANIFEST PRESENCE *of* GOD.

All rights reserved. No portion of this book may be reproduced, stored in a retrieval system, or transmitted in any form or by any means—electronic, mechanical, photocopy, recording, or other—except for brief quotations in printed reviews, without the prior written permission of the publisher.

Published in association with The Envoy Group, Colorado Springs, Colorado

Unless otherwise indicated, Scripture quotations in this volume are taken from the Holy Bible, New International Version (NIV). Copyright © 1973, 1978, 1984 by the International Bible Society. Used by permission of Zondervan Publishing House. All rights reserved. Other Scripture quotations are from the following sources:

Holy Bible New Living Translation (NLT), © 1996 by Tyndale Charitable Trust. Used by permission of Tyndale House Publishers.

Integrity Publishers and the author do not assume any risk or liability for the activity ideas expressed in the book. Careful research needs to precede any of these endeavors, as some do involve levels of risk.

Stories of the author's children are used by permission.

Names of some individuals in the illustrations have been changed to protect privacy. Scenarios may be a combination of individual stories to protect confidentiality.

Library of Congress Cataloging-in-Publication Data
Smith, Tim, 1954-
    The seven cries of today's teens : hearing their hearts, making the connection / by Timothy Smith.
        p. cm.
    ISBN 1-59145-050-0
    1. Teenagers—Life skills guides. 2. Teenagers—Conduct of life. 3. Parent and teenager. I. Title: Seven cries of teens. II. Title.

HQ796 .S5538 2002
305.235—dc21

2002038831

Printed in the United States of America
03 04 05 06 07 08 LBM 6 5 4 3 2 1

To Brooke

May you always be a refreshing source
of life and laughter.

Love, Dad

But if from there you seek the LORD your God, you will find him
if you look for him with all your heart and with all your soul.

DEUTERONOMY 4:29 NIV

Contents

Hope and Help for the Future

GEORGE GALLUP JR.

Tomorrow's world will be greatly affected by how we deal with youth today. Many trends give us real cause for pause. Young people are asking questions, and they're not getting answers.

Tim Smith's book, *The Seven Cries of Today's Teens*, is making a timely appearance. Tim is well equipped to write this book. In determining the Seven Cries, he has painstakingly examined the available research on the topic, both from experts and teens themselves. And he roots this information in his own direct, hands-on experience with families, which spans a quarter century.

It has been my pleasure to work with Tim on this project and as a Fellow with The George H. Gallup International Institute. We enjoy a long shared history of commitment to young people. The Gallup Youth Survey was founded twenty-five years ago to help society meet its responsibility to youth, by providing an ongoing reality check of what is on the hearts and minds of teens. During

1

this period more than twelve hundred weekly reports on youth have been released through the Associated Press. As a contribution to this book, the Gallup Youth Survey explored the vital needs of teens today in a customized, exclusive poll: the Gallup "Cries of Teens" Survey.

Tim Smith's goal in writing this book is to provide hope and practical help for parents and others who care about teenagers. His hope and prayer for the book is that it will be a tool to enhance the health of our adolescents—spiritual, emotional, and physical.

The word *cries* is the appropriate one to describe the voice of youth today: an utterance—even a primal yell—of an emotion such as fear or anger; an urgent entreaty or appeal; and, to some extent, a rallying call to fellow teenagers. The Seven Cries that Tim describes arise from anger, fear, anguish, confusion, and from deep needs.

Today's teenagers—the millennials—will be the leaders and shapers of the twenty-first century. Yet how much do we as a society know about this vital segment of the U.S. populace, which has the potential to lift our nation to new levels of achievement and social health? The image of teens in America today, surveys have revealed, is a negative one. Teens are frequently maligned, misunderstood, or simply ignored by their elders. Adjectives such as *immoral, reckless,* and *untrustworthy* are used to describe today's teenage population. Sadly, teens are aware adults view them in a negative light.

Yet a quarter century of the Gallup Youth Survey has provided ample evidence of the special qualities of the nation's youngsters. In fact, if our society is less racist, less sexist, less polluted, and more peace loving, we can, in considerable measure, thank our young people, who have been on the leading edge of these trends. And this is not a generation geared toward greed: Survey after survey has shown that teens have a keen interest in helping people less fortunate than themselves, especially in their own community.

Yet, despite the major impact teens are having on society—economically, socially, and in other ways—the sad truth is that *America is not meeting the needs of its children.* Children worry about their physical well-being. They are apprehensive about their future. Foremost among their concerns are AIDS, dangerous drugs, and random death and violence.

Six years of Gallup youth surveys identify ten recurring needs. These ten needs were put to a fresh sample of teens, to measure the relative strength of these needs in the minds of survey respondents. Large majorities cited each of the ten needs—that is, they chose category five ("very strong need") on a five-point scale.

That these cries are basic and fundamental human needs is evident in the fact that respondents choosing "very strong need" differ little in terms of characteristics such as age, sex, geographic region, level of income, and academic status.

We call the top seven needs *The Seven Cries of Today's Teens.* In order of frequency of mention, they are

- *The need to be trusted.* Teens believe that their elders distrust them and regard them as irresponsible and unpredictable. Teens want to be taken seriously.

- *The need to be understood and loved.* Teens tend to believe that their elders do not understand them. They crave to be listened to and loved by their parents or guardians.

- *The need to feel safe and secure* where they live and go to school. Sadly, this is not always the case.

- *The need to believe life is meaningful and has a purpose.* Surveys show that this is a growing need in the populace as a whole.

- *The need to be listened to—to be heard.* Teens have much to say, but are we listening?

✢ *The need to be appreciated and valued.* Roughly one-third of teens are found to have low self-esteem, which is, of course, a key factor in antisocial behavior.

✢ *The need to be supported in their efforts.* Teens want more help from their parents on homework and more discussion on a wide range of topics.

Gallup Youth Surveys underscore the compelling qualities of youth—their idealism, optimism, spontaneity, and exuberance. Young people tell us they are enthusiastic about helping others, willing to work for world peace and a healthy world, and feel positive about their schools and even more positive about their teachers.

Teens want clear rules to live by; they want clarity. They favor teaching values in schools, which half of the schools do now. In the area of sex education, teens overwhelmingly would like to have abstinence taught. Young women would like more help in knowing how to say no. Millennials would like to see divorce harder to get. They'd like to see more premarriage counseling. They overwhelmingly want to reduce the level of violence on television.

Nearly half of all our youth today volunteer. Half of all schools have a volunteer program. A majority of young people would like to see such programs made mandatory. (If a child is involved in volunteerism before age eleven, volunteering becomes a lifetime habit.) Youth seem to know what is best for themselves and for the nation. Then why aren't we listening to them?

Teens remain eternally optimistic, particularly about their personal futures. Yet they are apprehensive about the future of society and a host of problems that were not on the scene just a few decades ago.

In reality, teens today face a rough future—a future in which at least half of all marriages will break up, in which alcohol abuse and alcoholism will continue to ravage society, in which crime will remain at high levels. Unfortunately, this list of negative trends can be greatly extended.

American teens, therefore, need to be called upon, not simply to live up to social norms—to fit in—but to be the helpers and healers that will begin to turn our society around. We need to look to teens to transcend culture, not simply to adapt to it.

How do we prepare our youth to take on this role? How do we redeem the promise of our children? Indeed, is there a more important or pressing topic? Can anyone deny that our children need a greater share of our time, energy, and resources?

There is much to be done. A recent report from the Lutheran Brotherhood and Search Institute, based on a 2000 Gallup survey, notes: "We live in a society [where], despite widespread concerns about children and teenagers, the vast majority of adults are not actively involved in the lives of young people outside of their own families. This reality has a profound impact on community life and on young people's development. Without the attentions of many adults in all parts of their lives and community, young people are deprived of important sources of guidance, nurture, care, and socialization."

Yet there are in place wonderful success stories of programs that are working to keep youth from risks, mindful that teens should be regarded not as pathologies waiting to happen, but sparks of joy to be developed and nurtured. When people care about children enough to invest in their lives, something magical happens. We are seeing a trend toward hands-on, face-to-face kinds of volunteerism, including mentoring, direct contact between the privileged and the underprivileged, and broken-down walls of indifference. Nothing short of this will alleviate the social ills that affect our society. Nothing less is worthy of our children.

Inner-city youngsters, especially, live in an atmosphere that says, "You can't make it." They're surrounded by people who haven't made it. The messages they receive are relentlessly negative. These youth have a particular need for mature adults who can take them aside, give them a hug, and tell them, quietly and convincingly, an entirely different story.

Tim Smith's book calls for adults to listen anew to the cries of today's teens and to do so with a sense of urgency, for, as one social observer has noted, teens make up one-fifth of the population but one hundred percent of the future.

George Gallup Jr.
Princeton, New Jersey

INTRODUCTION

What's a *Millennial*?

Today's teens have been called the *millennial generation*—the generation emerging at the end of one millennium and the beginning of another, a generation of extremes.

Extreme sports are in. The X Games were made for the Extreme Generation: extreme in-line skating and vert ramp biking, extreme skateboarding and wakeboarding, extreme rock climbing and sky surfing. Perhaps the strongest image reflecting millennials is snowboarding. This extreme sport was born when they were. The fashion, the equipment, the language, the culture, the death-defying flips and in-your-face attitude capture the essence of millennials—at least one end of the millennial continuum.

At the other extreme we have teens who are committed to starting prayer groups on their campuses, who spend their Saturdays working in soup kitchens and their vacations teaching children in the inner cities or in foreign countries. And to make the whole topic more complex, some of these kids snowboard!

Millennials do not fit the traditional stereotypes we have for teenagers. They tend to be outside the "teenager" box, which is why they are often referred to as extreme. To some, they appear to be a paradox, talking about extreme sports one minute and serving Christ in some remote region the next.

Teen violence and angst have pierced our nation's soul. North American teens have captured our attention. Grief and haunting images arise at the mere mention of Littleton, Colorado; Pearl, Mississippi; West Paducah, Kentucky; Jonesboro, Arkansas; Springfield, Oregon. Tragically, the list goes on. While this may be the most violent generation of teens, it may also be the most spiritual. It is, after all, a generation of extremes. Because of this spiritual group, some refer to them as the *revival generation.*

What makes the difference between millennials who shoot up their schools and millennials who stand in circles of prayer at their schools? What can we do as parents, youth workers, and mentors to understand and positively impact the millennial generation?

The purpose of this book is to address these questions. I want to help you understand today's emerging youth culture and discover how to effectively relate to millennials.   .

A millennial is generally defined as a young person who was born during 1982 or after. The first millennials graduated in the high school class of 2000.

To get a grasp on the characteristics of this generation, I evaluated the last six years of research completed by The George H. Gallup International Institute gathered through the Gallup Youth Survey. The George H. Gallup International Institute, a nonprofit organization, was founded in 1988 in memory of a man who sought to develop opinion research as a tool for building an enlightened society. Its mission is "to discover, test, and encourage application of new approaches to social problems in education, environment, health, religion, and human values." I'm honored to be a Gallup Institute Fellow, a diverse group of men and women who seek to be agents of positive change in America. In addition to allowing me to review existing data, George Gallup Jr. graciously assisted me in designing and implementing a youth survey specifically for this book. Because of his support and generosity, I am able to write with confidence about the millennial generation. For more information, check out The Gallup Organization at *www.gallup.com.*

I have aimed to produce a book based on solid findings, not simply anecdotes and opinions. The scientific standards for and methodologies of research have been followed—the same standards and methodologies used in surveys for CNN, *Newsweek, USA Today,* and other media providers that partner with Gallup.

A Summary of the Research

Teenagers have captured our attention. Some adults report that teens are "worse than ever," while others are more upbeat and positive, calling today's teens "sincere, conservative, and spiritual." Since The Gallup Organization gave me exclusive access to its research, I discovered recurring issues, easily identifiable as important themes because of their status in the rankings and the frequency in which teenagers cited them. Additional exclusive research conducted for this book by Gallup undergirds the Seven Cries.

Out of these top issues, seven stood out dramatically from the rest. We call these *The Seven Cries of Today's Teens.* I define *cry* as a signal, a call for help or a demand for attention. It does not necessarily have to be a cry of sorrow or pain—but it will become that if no one responds. I'm using *cry* as a wake-up call. We need to pull ourselves away from distractions and hear the cries of the millennial generation.

What Are They Crying For?

"What do teens want? I have two at home, and I can't figure them out."

Todd was my host for a national morning drive-time radio talk show, and I was surprised by his question. Maybe because it was too early. Maybe because I needed another cup of coffee.

"I mean, are kids the same today as they were when we were teens?"

"In some ways they're just like us, and in some ways they're different. One thing that's drastically different is the culture. We live in a relativistic culture now. We don't agree on what's right and wrong. We live in a design-your-own-morality world."

"But what about the generation gap?" Todd inquired. "Does it still exist?"

"When we were teens, we were fighting to distinguish ourselves *from* our parents. Now teens are hoping they'll have dinner *with* their parents. The Generation Gap no longer exists—except in the minds of some parents. A recent Gallup Youth Survey indicates that about three out of four teens would like more time with their parents, not less."

"So they want to hang out with us?"

"No, not necessarily. They aren't likely to wander the mall with us holding our hands."

"Why is that? Why don't they want to be seen with us in public?"

"It's normal. Teens are in search of themselves. On their way, they need to become independent and separate from us. They're on a journey to discover the unique person God has made them. They aren't sure who this person is, but they know one thing: They don't want to be us!"

Todd didn't laugh but continued on his quest. "That's why I scheduled this interview. It seems that teens are destined to rebel or mess up their lives."

"Not necessarily. They give us warning signs and signals. Teens communicate to us what they need. If we respond to those needs, they're not as likely to rebel; they're more likely to make wise choices."

"What signs? Do you mean my teens might be sending me a signal and I don't even know it? Why can't I just parent the way my parents did?"

"Because it's a different world. Your teens are millennials. They're different."

I thought it was ironic that this nationally known talk-show host, highly regarded for his insight, was perplexed by his own teen-agers. I didn't say it, but I thought, *Our teens can make fools of us all!*

"How do we know what the signals are?"

"We discover the Seven Cries of today's teens and see them as indi-cators of our teens' needs. As loving parents, we seek to respond to their cries and fulfill many of their needs."

I introduced Todd to the Seven Cries of today's teens. We con-cluded the radio interview. And when it was over, I felt like Todd had gained a fresh perspective on his teenagers.

I hope this book does the same for you.

The Parent Question

As I worked on the manuscript for this book, I presented the findings to several parent groups. Invariably, somebody would ask, "How did you come up with seven? Aren't there more?"

"Sure, there are more than seven. In fact, our research indicates dozens of needs, but these are the top seven and all are remarkably higher than the others. They're valid in a variety of settings—urban, rural, suburban—and across the socioeconomic and educational spectrum. If we can deal with these seven with our teens, we'll be doing much to help our teens navigate adolescence."

"Aren't these the same needs that we had when we were teens?"

"Yes, in some ways, but the volume is much louder, just like today's stereos that can alter your heartbeat with the bass. They're so much more powerful than the tinny cassette players of our era. The stakes are higher now. The consequences are greater. If we ignored the needs of teens a decade ago, they might blow us off and go have a beer. If their needs are ignored now, they might blow us off with a gun."

"Why? Are kids worse off today?"

"Not necessarily. We have more resources and more parents trying to be effective parents. It's just that we have so many antifamily ele-ments in our culture. Many of these teens are growing up as children of divorce and with their moms at work. They come home to empty homes and most don't have positive adult role models, say, a grandparent or uncle or aunt they can look to. In fact, now it seems being pro-family isn't politically correct."

"Are the findings discouraging?"

"No. In spite of calling them *cries,* they aren't really the seven whines of today's teens. Think of them as being alarms or wake-up calls. The research indicates that a lot of our teens are doing very well, are optimistic, and more traditional."

"How can we respond to the Seven Cries?"

"Read *The Seven Cries of Today's Teens* and discuss it with other parents. Apply some of the practical suggestions offered in each chapter."

The Seven Cries of Today's Teens

A cry for trust
A cry for love
A cry for security
A cry for purpose
A cry to be heard
A cry to be valued
A cry for support

Who Are These Millennials?

In the last few years, our national attention has shifted toward the seventy million-plus kids also called *Generation Y.* Who are these kids born between 1982 and 2002? Are they the spoiled and jaded offspring of a society that is too busy, too affluent, and too narcissistic?

Not exactly. Millennials tend to be optimistic, self-reliant, ambitious, and discriminating about the deluge of messages that engulf them. They aren't caught up in the I'm-cooler-than-you credo that Generation X lived by. They *do* care, and they typically adopt traditional values of community, stability, home, family life, and education.

Our research offers insight into the practical and moral qualities of millennials and their goals for the future. They want to have well-paying jobs, respect from others, and good relationships with their parents. So the future is brighter than we thought. They want good relationships with us! (And we want them to get well-paying jobs to support us in our old age!)

Break Out the Poodle Skirts

In some ways, we are living the 1950s all over again. Millennials may be more like Ricky Nelson, Dobie Gillis, and Bud Anderson than the hippies of the '60s, the disco clubbers of the '70s, the yuppies of the '80s, and the New Agers of the '90s. Today's teens, like Ricky, Dobie, and Bud, are cheerful and optimistic, and they would appreciate a little more respect and guidance from caring adults. They aren't all the menacing, depressed psychos frequently portrayed by the mainstream media. They aren't looking to revolutionize the world or escape it. They are, in a word, *neotraditionalists*. They may look extreme with their haircuts, fashions, and penchant for the fringe, but deep inside is a longing for ideals to believe in, a purpose to pursue, and a family or group of friends to accompany them.

A millennial may look like a wild nonconformist, but underneath the bleached hair and the body piercing is a heart that is likely to be passionate about God, country, and family.

Our survey findings are reinforced by data from the U.S. Department of Education. Former Education Secretary Richard Riley spoke of the results: "They may dress differently, look different, and listen to music that is simply beyond us, but they are not a lost generation or a negative generation." Most teens are ambitious, striving, and open to the future. They reported that they are more likely to be bored (57 percent) than angry (37 percent), depressed (24 percent), or lonely (23 percent). When asked whom they turn to for support and guidance, a vast majority said they rely "a lot" or a "fair amount" on their

> Today's teens' views have changed since the GYS [Gallup Youth Survey] began 25 years ago. In fact, the change has been quite dramatic. One might say, "Here come the traditionalists." America's current high schools and the next age group [are] destined to make their mark on the American scene. Perhaps reacting to what might be described as the excesses of their parents' generation, teens today are decidedly more traditional than their elders were, in both lifestyles and attitudes. GYS data from the past 25 years reveal that teens today are far less likely than their parents were to use alcohol, tobacco, and marijuana. In addition, they are less likely than their parents even today to approve of sex before marriage and having children out of wedlock.
>
> —*Gallup Tuesday Briefing,* 30 July 2002

parents (78 percent) or friends (75 percent).[1]

We will discover that this is only part of the picture. It is not all cheery, and it is not all bleak. The accurate picture is somewhere in the middle (as it usually is).

The Common Denominator

Getting ahold of a conclusive understanding of millennials is a bit like trying to shoot Jell-O through a basketball hoop—it is theoretically possible but very difficult. On one hand, millennials seem optimistic and conservative; on the other hand, they appear to be morose and out of control. But one word is inclusive of today's teens:

Extreme

As I mentioned earlier, *extreme* is a concept that seems to work when we try to peg this generation. In the Christian pop group dc Talk's popular song "Jesus Freak," the singers ask

What will people think when they hear that I'm a Jesus Freak?
What will people do when they find that it's true?
I don't really care if they label me a Jesus Freak
There ain't no disguising the truth.

"I looked up the word *freak* [in the dictionary]," says band member Toby McKeehan. "It said 'an ardent enthusiast.' I realized that being a Jesus freak is deeper than being an ardent enthusiast. These are the ultimate Jesus freaks—the people who are willing to die for their faith. When you look at the killings at Wedgwood Baptist Church and Columbine, I believe that people are going to have to start counting the cost of saying, 'I'm a Christian.' *This generation is into extremes.* There are extreme sports, and Hollywood is into throwing extremes at us. I believe that Christians will live up to these extremes because that is what the culture calls for. As believers, we need to be just as potent."[2]

Another word describing millennials might be *intensity.*

"There's an intensity among the Christians that wasn't there when I was younger," dc Talk singer Michael Tait says of fans attending his band's concerts. "It almost dumbfounds me. These guys are fifteen and sixteen years old and serious about their faith. At the same time, it shows you your true colors."[3]

I have worked with youth since 1974, and I have never seen a group of teens so extreme, so intense, and so diverse. Some of them demonstrate courage, tenacity, and commitment that I—a much older adult—don't have. They are mirroring values from the 1950s, more like the G. I. Generation of their grandparents. In response to the terrorist attacks on the World Trade Center and Pentagon, millennials responded with patriotism and a zeal for justice, much like their grandparents did during World War II. Millennials will be our new heroes.

According to authors Neil Howe and William Strauss, millennials will "enter their teens looking and behaving better than any in decades. . . . This generation will build a reputation for meeting and beating adult expectations."[4]

These two respected sociologists have made predictions that have proven to be accurate. Clothing and music trends are brighter and happier, peer pressure has become a positive force, adolescent crime has dropped, and romance (instead of fast sex) has returned to relationships. Swing dancing has made a huge resurgence. Teenage pregnancies and abortions have dropped, and there is a trend toward early marriage.

Millennials are appropriately labeled *neotraditionalists* for other reasons as well. They are more likely than their parents to say that raising a family and being well off financially are very important. In fact, millennials choose to go to college to make more money and to prepare for graduate school. With all of this going for them, it seems that life would be serene, but millennials face more serious problems than their parents did at this age (and possibly even now): the breakdown of the family, the long-term impact of divorce, AIDS, violence, crime, and the growing chasm between the lower class and the rising middle class.

MTV has homogenized regional differences. It used to be that teens in Texas liked a certain TV show and wore a particular brand of jeans—different from the kids in California or Michigan. Now they all take their cues from MTV. As I travel across the country, I notice that the regional differences have been minimized. Teens are likely to dress alike, talk alike, and value the same things, largely based on the kind of music they listen to. Hip hoppers in Texas look like those in Michigan. Top 40 kids in North Carolina mix in well with those from New Mexico. Music drives youth culture more than where they live. Millennials live in a world that's much less ethnically isolated than their parents did when they were teens. Peter Zollo of Teenage Research Unlimited says, "Minority teen culture has an incredible influence on white teens."[5] Baggy jeans, oversized jersey tops, basketball shoes, and gold jewelry were at one time restricted to the rappers, but now they are mainstream, thanks to the popularity of hip hop and dance music.

Because they value diversity, millennials are willing to cross over former barriers of race, religion, and alternative lifestyles. This crossover mentality can be seen in their music. Country and pop music à la Dixie Chicks and Faith Hill is currently popular with some teens. The same is true of some rap/hip hop/dance music. Music used to be more strictly categorized; now music is becoming more eclectic. Some groups like to sample "old school" music from the '70s into their new projects. Millennials like the variety. They like the buffet approach to their entertainment: a little something new, mixed with something from another style, with a sample from a cool sound from a previous era, all mixed together with their favorite beat.

The following chart compares and contrasts three generations.

Boomers, Gen Xers, and Millennials

Boomers	Gen Xers	Millennials
Prefer black and white moral values	Value a gray world— no absolutes	Comfortable with paradox— prefer black and white
Are idealistic	Are cynical	Are optimistic
Value people's words	Value people's actions	Value people (community)
Value what's right	Value what's real	Value teamwork
Make choices based on passion	Make choices based on what is real and practical	Make choices based on changing criteria
Focus on philosophies	Focus on results	Focus on social change
See conformity as unity	See diversity as unity	Consider conformity outdated
Value causes	Value relationships	Value productive relationships
Focus on the group	Focus on the individual	Focus on survival and success of self
Find meaning in abstract thought	Find meaning in what they can experience with their senses	Find meaning in controlling useful information
Live to work	Work to live	Live to know
Returned to faith when they became parents	Are "Spiritual Sensors"	Are "Spiritual Questers"

I will go into more detail about the characteristics of millennials in the following chapters. The twelve generation descriptors in the chart are general. Some millennials may reflect some aspects of the Gen X list, particularly if they are older. Millennials and Gen Xers share many common traits:

- They are comfortable with contradictions.

- They are highly relational.

- They harbor feelings of abandonment.

- They have a great interest in spirituality.

- They endure massive exposure to media.

- They seek comfort without having to sell out their values.

- They highly value family.

- They are confused regarding the purpose of life.

- They accept change as a constant in life.

- Technology is a natural part of their existence.

The Seven Cries of Today's Teens Summarized

A CRY FOR TRUST

Millennials have a fairly clear idea of what they want in the future, but they don't know how to get there or who will help them. Most are open to a closer relationship with their parents, or a mentor, or both. They aren't as cynical as their Gen X brothers and sisters. They are willing to trust someone, but they aren't sure what that looks like. After all, trust is a critical element of marriage, and these are children of divorce. They are open to giving trust a chance, but they are looking for models of trust. They are ambitious enough to succeed, but they are confused about the meaning, purpose, and direction of life. They need trusted guides who know the way, but for many, no adults are around to protect them or show them the way.

A CRY FOR LOVE

We discovered that many teens do not feel loved even though their parents say *I love you* or give them hugs on a regular basis. In order to feel loved, they need to experience love in *their* love key (see pages 52–69 for a comprehensive explanation of love keys). Some of this does not seem logical to parents—and that is the point. Successfully relating to teenagers is not logic-based. You can't always think your way out of a problem with your teenager or reason your way into a closer relationship. Sometimes with millennials, you are better to *feel* your way.

A CRY FOR SECURITY

Immediately after the terrorist attacks of September 11, 2001, I counseled many teens who were rattled by the trauma of what they saw on TV. In some cases, teens were more stressed than younger children. This could be because teens often believe the myth that they are immortal. When they saw reality TV of planes crashing into towers and people jumping from burning buildings, their I-will-always-be-safe world crumbled.

In spite of the recent terrorism and school shootings, most teens feel safe. Teens are looking for borders. Borders protect our teens and allow them to be relatively carefree as they pass through their last stage of childhood. Teenagers are frightened to live in a culture that doesn't protect them, hurries them into adulthood and adult-sized problems, and doesn't equip them to handle adult problems.

A CRY FOR PURPOSE

Our teens need to believe that life is meaningful and has a purpose. When teens feel that their lives are purposeful, they feel more capable and equipped to take on the demands of adolescence. Purpose is developed as teens discover the Three D's of Purpose:

Design God made each of us according to His master plan.
Destiny We discover our purpose in relationship to God.
Duty Our purpose is further developed as we discover what we can offer in service to God and others.

One cause of the lack of purpose is that many teens do not take time to reflect. Their active schedules and the clamor of the media crowd out time for serious reflection. As a result, teens make decisions with a *mosaic morality*—a little of this combined with a little of that. Millennials desire meaning and morals, but they don't often have the time, energy, and examples to build an integrated moral base. Since they make decisions based on ever-changing criteria, they are often disappointed with the results.

A CRY TO BE HEARD

Millennials are very comfortable living in today's Information Age. Technology is as familiar to them as their pacifiers were. Yet, in the midst of this torrent of input, their voice is drowned out. Many millennials feel they "don't have a voice" and want to be heard above the noise. They have high hopes for the future but feel "so-so" about the present. Most teens would welcome a serious discussion with a caring adult. They are eager to share their opinions and are looking for compassionate adults to interact with. Millennials are crying to be listened to.

A Cry to Be Valued

We live in a culture that is increasingly antichildren. Boomer parents, on the road to success, have sometimes embraced the values of the culture over the value of addressing their teens' needs. Many of our teens feel alone. They haven't pulled away from their parents as much as their parents have pulled away from them, leaving them *a tribe apart* (as Patricia Hersch describes them in her book of the same title). How will our teens discover, test, and embrace the values that are important to us if we aren't around to pass them along?

Our teens are generally doing well. They are in the right place at the right time, but they aren't coming to the right conclusions. They need mentors and guides to protect them and to help them process ideas and shape values. Our teens are looking for rites of passage that affirm their progress as they develop.

A Cry for Support

The African proverb, "It takes a village to raise a child," could be adapted to say, "It takes a community network to raise a teenager." Our teens are eager for support. They are quick to admit that they need it. They want to be connected and are open to learn from those who have gone before. They want to be included and to make a difference. They feel supported when they are included in our processes and allowed some autonomy to make decisions. Because of our culture, teens are more at risk. We need to compensate by developing networks that build community and help our youth. We need partnerships between parents and schools, between businesses and after-school programs, between the private and public sectors, and between the church and home. We need to strategically plan support for our teens, because many of them feel that we spend all our efforts at work and that we have little to offer them in their aspirations.

The Cries of Young People Today

Results from the exclusive Gallup "Cries of Teens" Survey

Findings are based on telephone interviews with 501 persons, aged 13–17, nationwide.

Question: *I am going to read some needs of young people today. Please tell me how you feel with "one" being not a need at all and "five" being a very strong need in your life today.*

National percentage totals for the answers "strong need" (four) and "very strong need" (five), ranked in order according to total answers in those two categories.

Cry	Percentage
1. The need to be trusted	92.7
2. The need to be understood and loved	92.2
3. The need to feel safe and secure where I live and go to school	92.1
4. The need to believe that life is meaningful and has purpose	91.6
5. The need to be listened to, to be heard	91.5
6. The need to be appreciated or valued	88.2
7. The need to be supported in my efforts	87.4

My prayer is that this book will inform you about the need to connect with your teenager and inspire you to work at it. Our culture races along with shocking images bombarding our teens. They have learned to cope by operating in extremes. To them, what they experience is normal. The blurring of the boundaries makes them want clarity and decisiveness. Their spiritual longing prepares them to be devoted in their quest for God. It is time for parents and youth workers to seize the day—to capture our teens while they are seeking God, to build trust, express love, and provide a safe place to help our teens discover purpose and meaning. Our teens are crying out.

Will you respond?

CHAPTER 1

A Cry for Trust

Mom, this is my friend Dominick. Can we give him a ride home?" Ryan pleaded as he looked through the open car door. "He lives by us."

"Uh, sure, Ryan. Hop in, Dominick. Nice to meet you." Audrey was caught off-guard by her son's new friend. He was wearing a leather vest and a T-shirt with the sleeves cut off, exposing two huge tattoos, one on each arm.

"Thanks, Mrs. Hopper. I appreciate it."

"No problem." Audrey double-checked the minivan's side mirror as she rolled through the high school parking lot, dodging and braking as teenagers scurried in circles around the vehicles. It was like a video game. Try to get out of the lot without running over a high school student or having one hit you with his car as he speeds through the lot showing off his two-month-old driving skills. Today Audrey scored 500 points—no hits or scrapes. As she pulled into the street, she checked the rearview mirror. *Dominick has earrings and a nose stud! Why is Ryan hanging out with him?*

Dominick caught her eye in the mirror and smiled. "Hey, Ryan, how about some tunes?"

As he talked, she caught sight of flashing metal in his mouth. *Dominick's tongue was pierced too. Gross! Where did Ryan meet this guy?* "So, Ryan, how did you guys meet?"

"In P.E. We have lockers close to each other." Ryan fiddled with the stereo.

"Dominick, have you lived here long? I haven't seen you around."

"Since middle school. I've never had a class with Ryan before, but I've been around."

"Do you do any sports or anything after school?"

"Nah, I'm not much of a jock, like Ryan here," he flexed his arm and smiled at Ryan, who was riding shotgun.

"What do you like to do?"

Ryan winced; he could tell his mom was in her classic F.B.I. (Family Bureau of Investigation) mode. He cleared his throat, but she ignored him.

Dominick smiled at Ryan and raised his eyebrows. "Well, let's say I like to rock and roll." He emitted a tiny chuckle as he said *roll*.

Drugs! Addict! Loser! Drugs! The words circled within Audrey's brain. *He certainly looks like a druggie. He has no sports or anything to keep him busy. Oh my goodness. My son is friends with a drug user!* She composed herself long enough to ask, "Oh, so you are in the band?"

"Not the band at school, Mom. I'm sure!" corrected Ryan. He and Dominick laughed as they imagined Dominick in the school marching band.

"No, Mrs. Hopper, I'm not in the marvelous marching Mustangs," mocked Dominick.

"Mom, the school band is for losers. Dominick is in a cool rock band. They call it *Blade*."

Audrey tried to regroup as she guided the minivan around the corner. Somehow her son had a knack for making her feel stupid. It irritated her. "Since when are bands and sports for losers?"

"I didn't say sports was for losers, just that the geeky 'marching on the field at halftime wearing weird costumes deal' is."

"So people in rock bands don't have costumes?" The sarcasm dripped off her tongue as she checked out Dominick's response in the mirror.

"I guess we do, but the difference is we choose them, not some band director from a decade ago."

"Yeah, Mom. Blade is touring, and they've already cut a CD."

"The next Backstreet Boys, I'm sure."

Ryan was offended by his mother's sarcasm and subtle putdown, but Dominick wanted to spar with her.

"Oh, we don't do that sissy stuff. We're straight rock and roll. You know, classic rock. Stuff from your time."

They dropped Dominick off at his house and drove home in silence. Finally, Audrey broke the stillness. "Do you know Dominick very well?"

"Yeah, pretty well. He's a lot of fun."

"He's different from your other friends."

"Yeah, that's what I like. He's not boring."

"Is he really into the rock-and-roll scene?"

"Yeah, he wants to do it full time after he graduates this year."

"Graduates? Will he pass his classes?"

"Mom!" Irritated, Ryan shifted in his seat to face her. "Dominick is in honors classes. He gets straight A's and has universities after him."

"He looks like a druggie."

"You are so judgmental. You don't even know him."

"He has tattoos and a nose ring."

"It's the style. Do you want him to look preppy and be in a rock band?"

"I don't want you to see him anymore, Ryan. He's trouble."

"What? Have you gone completely crazy? You can't tell me who my friends are. I am almost seventeen! What have you been smoking?"

"It's what that tongue-stud pal of yours has been smoking that worries me. I forbid you to see him anymore!"

"*Forbid?* When did you start to sample Shakespeare? I beseech ye to forsake thy troublesome companion. You've flipped!" He turned away from her and stared out the window.

"Oh, you're overreacting! You have plenty of other friends. Why don't you invite Jim over to play video games? You haven't had him over for months."

Silence. Ryan retreated into his own world and had no intention of coming out for anyone—especially his annoying mother.

The Biggest Need

Sound familiar? Have you ever tried to enter your teen's world only to be rebuffed? Finding balance is tricky. If we show too much interest, our teens feel we are investigating. If we show too little interest, they conclude that we don't care. Raising teens requires finesse—the fine act of knowing when to get involved and when to walk away. At the core of this balance is trust. Teenagers desperately want our trust. According to our exclusive Gallup Youth Survey, the need to be trusted is the biggest need among today's adolescents. Ninety-three percent reported trust is a "very strong" or "strong" need in their lives. You might have guessed another need would take first place—the need for love or for friends—but in the teenager's economy

Trust = Freedom

Teens reason, *If your parents trust you, you'll have more freedom.* Plus, teenagers like to feel that they can be trusted, that they are responsible, capable, and honest. But sometimes we find it difficult to trust our teens. They aren't responsible. They aren't capable. They aren't honest. But they still want us to trust them. They still want the freedom that goes with trust, even though they haven't earned the trust.

What Is Trust?

Most teens feel insecure about relationships. They simply have not had that much experience with them. They aren't sure how much to give, what to say, or how much to take in a relationship. As a result, teens have difficulty establishing trust.

Trust is the key to effective relationships. It could be defined by this formula:

Trust = Truth Applied to Relationship

Trust occurs in a relationship when truth is the foundation. Parents are more likely to trust their teens when they know the truth about them. Teens are more likely to trust their parents when they know the truth about them. Pretending and dishonesty get in the way of healthy relationships.

One of the goals for this book is to help parents obtain an accurate view of what is happening with today's teens, the millennium generation. Looking at what thousands of teens are facing is likely to help you capture what is occurring with your teenager. I commend you for taking the time to understand what is going on inside the world of your teen. If you know the truth about your teens, you are more apt to trust them, but if you are unsure about what is actually happening with your teen, you are more likely to be suspicious and distrustful. One way you can enhance the trust in your parent-teen relationship is to find out more about today's teens.

For instance, we will discover that millennials aren't as cynical and aloof as busters. They desire authentic relationships forged on trust. Millennials want to connect with their parents and other adults. This may surprise you because many of us have been influenced to believe that teens want to be left alone. This is not entirely true. They don't want to hang out with us on Friday nights, but they do want time to talk with us and build a relationship of trust. They just don't know how.

The first cry of the millennials is an appeal for trust. Five trust robbers provoke teens and steal trust.

Five Ways to Frustrate Your Teen

> Fathers, do not exasperate your children; instead, bring them up in the training and instruction of the Lord. (Ephesians 6:4 NIV)

What does it mean to *exasperate* our teens? One common definition is to *frustrate* them. We get frustrated when somebody stands in the way of our goals. Our teens get frustrated when we relate to them in ways that provoke them. The Latin root of the word *exasperate* comes from *aspirate,* meaning to help breathe or add oxygen. The prefix *ex* means to take out. Therefore, *exasperate* originally meant to take the wind out of someone.

Remember when you fell on the playground and got the wind knocked out of you? Did it help that your friend came over and asked, "What's wrong?" Did you need a lecture from the teacher about swinging too high? What did you need?

Air, right?

When the wind gets knocked out of you, you don't need questions, lectures, or warnings. You need air.

The same thing is true of our teens. Sometimes we knock the wind out of them. We steamroll over them and crush their spirits. When we exasperate our teens, we rob them of their desire. We extinguish their motivation. That is why God warns us in Scripture not to exasperate our kids but instead to bring them up in the training and instruction of the Lord.

We exasperate our teens in these five ways:

1) *Judging teens by appearances or by what the media presents to us.* Audrey judged Dominick by his appearance. He seemed to be wild and a "druggie" based on what she had experienced and seen in the

media. But Dominick was not a substance abuser, and Ryan was frustrated by his mother's prejudice. Tolerance and acceptance are important values to millennials. Judging without really knowing someone is considered wrong.

2) *Sarcasm and put-downs.* Even if a comment is meant to be funny, coming from an adult, sarcasm and put-downs carry the risk of being taken as disapproval. You may say, "That shirt fits you like a tent." But your teen hears, "They think I don't know how to dress." Ryan was angry at his mom for her sarcastic comment about Dominick's band. Sarcasm might have worked better with boomers and older Gen Xers as a form of humor, but to most millennials, sarcasm is taken as disapproval or condescension.

3) *Expecting teens to act like adults because they look like adults.* Teens may have mature bodies, but their emotions and thinking may take some time to catch up. Expecting teens to live up to adult expectations creates frustration. Sometimes they need to express emotions more like a child than an adult.

4) *Minimizing feelings.* Audrey fell into this trap when she didn't consider her son's assessment and loyalty to his friend Dominick. She discounted that he would be able to make a wise choice and be loyal to it. Sometimes adults are not comfortable with the sweeping range of emotions teens have, so they write off the emotions. Instead of helping teens process and understand their feelings, adults minimize them. This feels condescending to teens and frustrates them.

5) *Assuming that what worked before will work now.* Audrey exasperated her son when she forbade him from seeing Dominick. To add insult to injury, she went to an old and ineffective tool of returning to what used to work: she suggested playing video games with Jim. This frustrates teens because it indicates that parents do not have a clue about what their teens currently want or who they have become. Treating teens like children and trying to regulate their friendships the way first graders are treated is a recipe for exasperation and is guaranteed to erode trust.

I like what family counselor John Rosemond writes on the topic of agitating our teens: "In short, we're thrusting children today into the most vulnerable period of their lives having deprived them of the defenses they will need to make sound decisions, while at the same time bombarding them with a host of temptations. Inadequate moral, emotional, intellectual, and behavioral defenses render anyone, much less a child, highly susceptible to intense feelings of insecurity."[1]

> How do we respond to the cry for trust? I believe we need to give teens the opportunity to be trusted. Surveys reveal that many adults misunderstand and malign teenagers, dismissing them as unruly, irresponsible, and misguided. Remedial action and new partnerships between older and younger Americans should be undertaken with a new urgency, to bring Americans of all ages together and restore a vital sense of community. Our young people binding us together as a nation—what an exhilarating thought!
>
> —*Gallup Tuesday Briefing,* 30 July 2002, adapted

What Teens Want in Their Parents

"Parents of teenagers face a difficult dilemma: how to help when help is resented, how to guide when guidance is rejected, how to communicate when attention is taken as attack."[2] Psychologist Haim Ginott captured the dilemma perfectly with that statement. Rearing a teenager requires skills and finesse and raises the question, "What do teens want in their parents?"

In *Understanding Today's Youth Culture,* Walt Mueller reports that teens were asked what they wanted most from their parents. Here are the top ten answers:

Teens want parents who . . .

- Don't argue in front of them

- Treat each family member the same

- Are honest

- Are tolerant of others

- Welcome their friends into the home

- Build a team spirit among their children

- Answer their questions

- Give punishment when needed, but not in front of others, especially their friends

- Concentrate on strengths instead of weaknesses

- Are consistent[3]

You can do everything on this list—read books, join groups, listen to tapes, and commit to being the best parent you can be—and still have a child who does not cooperate! Consider Rosemond's additional advice:

> Parents can do the right thing, and things may still go wrong—for a time at least. Or, maybe forever. Who knows? This idea—that with proper parenting, everything during the teen years will go smoothly—is "between the lines" of many a book and article on teens. It is—hear me clearly—so patently absurd as to make one wonder how otherwise intelligent people (the authors of those books and articles) could even suggest it. It implies not only that parents are omnipotent but also a

child bears no responsibility for the direction and tone of the parent/child relationship. . . . A child is not putty in his parents' hands any more than an employee is putty in an employer's hands. A human child is an independent agent (another way of saying he has a mind of his own). Being human, he is imperfect—in theological terms, *sinful*. He is not imperfect/sinful *because* of his parents; rather he is imperfect *because he is human*. For all these reasons, a child is completely capable, at an early age, of doing things that bear little relationship to how well (or how poorly) by some standard he has been "parented." Parenting is not sculpting: it is management . . . *good parenting does not guarantee a good outcome.*[4]

False Expectations

Maybe one of the reasons teens do not get along with parents is because we *expect* them not to. Parents of today's teens grew up in the turbulent '60s and '70s. The generation gap between parents and teens was widening. Today this gap does not exist. Gallup reports:

The generation gap that plagued families in the 1960s has all but disappeared. The great majority of teenagers now say they get along at least fairly well with their parents, although they more often get along better with Mom than with Dad. Relations often are better yet between teens and their grandparents. The majority of teens (54 percent) say they get along with their parents "very well," and an additional 43 percent report their relationships to be going "fairly well." Just 2 percent of teens say relations with their parents have deteriorated to a point where they do not get along at all well.[5]

If we expect to have conflict with our teens, we are likely to have it. If we expect them to rebel, they are likely to do it. If we expect our teens to develop conflict-resolution skills, they are likely to develop them. If we expect them to resolve issues, they are likely to do so. Our teens tend to live up to our expectations—good or bad.

An urban myth says, "All teens rebel. It's what they do." Another is, "Your teen is on the other side of the gap, and you can't reach him. You are destined to be alienated."

I don't buy either myth.

We will have conflict with our teens, as we will in most close human relationships. But it doesn't have to be worse than relationships with adults. In other words, a parent-teen relationship isn't destined for misery and pain. Also, you don't have to be alienated from your teenage son or daughter.

I am bothered when parents lament, "Yeah, she's eleven now. I better enjoy these last few years before she turns into a teenager," as if she were going to evolve into some hideous monster. Not all teenagers are rebellious, substance-abusing maniacs who carry automatic weapons to school.

Our children have a tendency to live up or down to our expectations. We need to have high—but not unrealistic—expectations for them. We improve the odds of favorable parent-teen relationships when we are positive and help our teens navigate adolescence rather than wringing our hands and worrying about every blemish.

Our kids are looking to us for cues on how to manage their teen years. If we give them a you-can-do-it, hey-try-this approach, the process is likely to be more enjoyable for them and us.

I love teenagers. I choose to spend my life with them. I wasn't worried about our daughters becoming teens. I just figured that I would try to relate to them like I had with other teens. (Every parent should be involved in youth ministry. Experiment with other people's teens before you have your own!) I expected to have fun with and relate well with our teenagers, and for most of the time, that has been true. Nobody ever bats a thousand. Whoever says he does is either lying or in a deep state of denial!

If you are nervous about relating to your teenager, remember one thing: *He or she is more like you than you care to admit.*

The Forty-Year-Old Adolescent

I like to call parents of teens forty-year-old adolescents. They generally do not like it, but it's descriptive for many. My theory is that parents and teens face common life-stage issues at the same time.

For instance, physically teens are discovering they are stronger, faster, and bigger than they were as children. Meanwhile, their parents are discovering that they are weaker, slower, wider, and shorter.

Emotionally, teens are experiencing a wide menu of human feelings, sometimes in one afternoon. Their parents are facing emotional issues: fear, anger, rejection, insecurity, and performance problems—before they even get to work.

Teens are inquisitive about their sexuality. They are excited about their new "equipment" and eager to try it out. Parents are also concerned about their own sexuality: They wonder where it went!

Teens are concerned about their families. In spite of your personal experience, teens actually think about and are concerned about their families. Parents are also concerned about their families. (That is why you are reading this book now.)

Teens are optimistic about the future and overwhelmed by the choices. Meanwhile, their parents may be worried about the future and the rapid decline of the choices they have.

Your teen's surge forward may conflict with your midlife assessment, but you both are dealing with the same basic issues. You may be asking the same questions as your teen:

❖ Who am I?

❖ Where do I belong?

✥ What am I good at?

✥ How capable am I?

✥ What will the future be?

✥ Who will I spend the future with?

Right at the time we need to be understanding and supportive of our teens, we often get nailed with our own adolescent-like issues. I think God designed it that way to make us more sensitive and understanding of our teens.

So instead of fighting these developmental issues, embrace them and talk about them with your teenager. You have more in common than you think. Adolescence is a time for change for both parent and child. Talking about these changes will enhance trust in your parent-teen relationship.

Trust-Training Your Teen

To build trust in our relationships with teens, we need to avoid the trust-robbers that destroy their spirits, and we need to offer them guidance that is based on God's Word. Remember Ephesians 6:4: "Do not exasperate your children; instead, bring them up in the training and instruction of the Lord." Our God-given role as parents is to train and instruct our children.

Training implies repetitive physical and visual demonstrations. You cannot train your child to ride a bike with books, videos, and lectures; you must get her outside and on a bike if she is to learn. You may begin with training wheels, but soon the day arrives when you take them off and run alongside her, holding the seat as she wobbles down the sidewalk. When she has her balance, you let go, and with screams of delight she rides away.

We need to train our teens in the same way. We use training

wheels to get them started; soon we run alongside them and let them go. They may fall. They may skin their knees. But training involves risk and failure. Unless we are willing to let them ride on their own, they will never learn. When we take time to train our teens, we show our trust. It could be something as simple as how to wash a car, how to balance a checkbook, or how to cook a favorite meal. To train our teens "of the Lord," we model for them how we worship, how we serve, and how we have a quiet time of prayer and of study in God's Word.

Instruction is more formal than training. It implies an academic approach to learning. Our teens need to know certain things to make wise decisions and to be able to navigate life. When we prepare our teens for life through instruction, we show our trust. We send a message: *I believe in you. You can do this. You are capable.*

One of the critical skills our teens need is the ability to resolve conflict. If we can help our teens learn to resolve conflict in their relationships, we will provide them with a skill that promotes trust.

How Conflict Can Aid Trust

Healthy families have discovered healthy ways to deal with conflict. Unhealthy families hide conflict or pretend it does not exist. With teenagers, you *will* have conflict. Prepare them for life by teaching them how to deal with it. Imagine how many relational problems your teens will be able to resolve if they can appropriately deal with conflict. We can equip our teens for successful marriages and lower the odds of divorce if we teach them to process their conflicts.

Sometimes we are not even aware of the sources of conflict with our teens. We just know something is wrong. We become agitated when our teenagers enter the room. Their voices grate on our nerves. Their music gets more annoying. These are signs of conflict. To help you assess conflict, have a piece of pie, Conflict Pie (see next page).

One of the most helpful steps in reducing conflict is to understand

Conflict Pie

Divide the circle into pie-shaped wedges that reflect the greater and smaller areas of conflict in your parent/teen relationship. If you have many areas of conflict, you may want to focus on the main ones only. Label each piece of the pie according to the particular conflict it represents, and size it according to the intensity of that category's conflict. You can use the categories listed below or create your own.

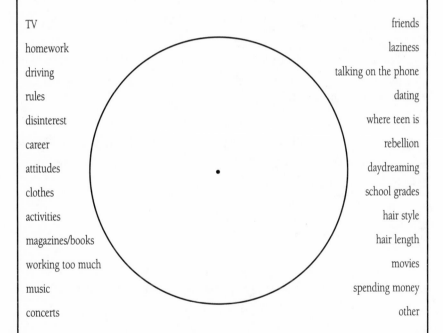

TV	friends
homework	laziness
driving	talking on the phone
rules	dating
disinterest	where teen is
career	rebellion
attitudes	daydreaming
clothes	school grades
activities	hair style
magazines/books	hair length
working too much	movies
music	spending money
concerts	other

A reproducible version of Conflict Pie can be found in Appendix A (page 227). You may make copies to write on.

where it comes from. Often we experience conflict but have not taken time to assess the source, so once you've filled in the Pie, discuss the results together. What are the three largest pieces of Conflict Pie? What are possible solutions for each of these?

When we discuss areas of conflict, our teens will be angry; we will be angry. We need to find ways to express anger and resolve conflict that won't hide the emotion or be destructive. Conflict is not a sin. In fact, it can refine us and develop character that we would not have had without experiencing the struggle. Some parents get discouraged because they don't know how to resolve conflict with their teens. The challenge is resolving it without exasperating or overcorrecting our teens.

The best way to deal with conflict is to talk with your teen ahead of time about how to argue or disagree. Establish some guidelines on how to fight fairly, for instance: no screaming, no name calling, and setting a time to deal with the issue in private and without being rushed. All families have conflict. Healthy families have a plan to resolve it when it comes up. This will help you grow together and learn from conflict, rather than create distance in your relationship.

Trust—Given or Earned?

"How can I trust her after what she has done?" asked Jasmine Bailey as she dabbed the corners of her eyes. "I never expected this. We're Christians, and we've always talked to our kids about drugs and alcohol. Now this!"

I tried to encourage her. "I know you have."

A small smile briefly appeared on her tear-streaked face. "I'm ashamed of LaShauna's behavior. I never expected her to go to a wild party and get drunk. Did we do something wrong? Are we bad parents?"

"You can do everything right and still have a teen who chooses to do something foolish or wrong." This didn't appear to comfort her.

"Well, what am I supposed to do? She's ruined my trust in her."

I tried to comfort Mrs. Bailey as she sat in my office, troubled by last weekend's incident with her sixteen-year-old daughter. "Trust is both given and earned. There are times when you say, 'Your behavior has lowered my trust in you, so you'll have to earn it back. You'll have to prove to me that you can be trusted.' But there are other times when we simply have to give trust. Our teens need a certain amount of trust to be free to make decisions. If we take all of their liberty away, we remove all of their choices and they can't earn back their trust. So sometimes we have to give them a little trust and freedom even though they don't deserve it."

"So I need to tell LaShauna that because of her behavior, there will be a consequence, but that I will give her enough leash that she can move a little and not be cooped up in her room for a month."

"Exactly. I think you got it," I said. "There's a loss of freedom due to her behavior, but not so much that there is also a loss of hope. You're telling LaShauna you believe in her, you forgive her, and you have confidence that she'll learn from this incident."

"Wow, that sounds so reasonable."

"Of course! It's not my kid!"

She smiled. "Honestly, where did you come up with the idea that trust is both given and earned?"

"It's right out of the Bible. God loved us so much that He gave us His son. He entrusted His most precious possession to us, and we rejected him. But God didn't say, 'You losers!' and alienate us from Him. Instead, He told us there would be consequences for our sin, but there was also forgiveness and a way back. That's what grace is all about. Grace is love in relationship. Grace is God's way of giving us trust when we don't deserve it. Grace-based parenting does the same thing."

"Ummh . . . I like that idea, *grace-based parenting*. It seems like the focus is on building trust rather than punishing the bad deed."

"That's right. It focuses on our teens' hearts, not just their behavior."

Discussion Questions

PARENT TO PARENT

1. Have you had an experience similar to Audrey's experience with her son's new friend Dominick? How did you handle it?

2. Which of the five ways to frustrate your teen (pages 28–29) is the easiest for you to fall into? How might you avoid it in the future?

3. Look at the list of top ten things teens want from their parents on page 31. Why do you think each is on the list?

4. Discuss John Rosemond's statement, "Good parenting does not guarantee a good outcome."

5. What are the common sources of conflict in your parent-teen relationships?

TALKING WITH YOUR TEEN

1. Show your teen the "five ways to frustrate" material on pages 28–29. Ask him for examples of each.

2. Ask your teen, "What are effective ways for me to help motivate you?"

3. Review the top ten things teens want in a parent (page 31). Ask your teen to make her own list. Discuss and compare lists.

4. Make a copy of the Conflict Pie for your teen (page 227). Have him fill it out. Discuss it together.

5. Choose one of the ideas in Trust-Building Ideas for Parents and Teens (pages 44–45) and do it.

Responding to the Cry

THE CRY

The cry for trust.

THE CHALLENGE

To trust our teens when we do not feel they are ready for the corresponding privileges.

TOOLS TO USE AT HOME

1. Make two charts with TRUST on one half of each and DISTRUST on the other. Give a copy to your teen and keep one for yourself. Make a list under each heading of what makes you trust or distrust the other age group (parents write about teens, teens write about parents). For example, under DISTRUST, parents might write "Teens with body piercings." Take a few minutes to discuss your lists. Ask questions like, "Why does [name the item] make you less trusting of me?"

2. Make some sandcastles together. If you aren't near the beach or lake, get some sand from a home improvement center. After you are done building, take a bucket of water and pour a small amount of it near the foundation of your castle.

   Talk about how truth is the foundation of all relationships. When we don't have truth, we can't have trust. When we lose trust, it erodes the foundation of relationship. A relationship can withstand some erosion, like a small amount of water.

   Pour in some more water. Point out how the castle becomes fragile when the foundation is eroded. The same is true of our relationships. Truth cements the trust and lies erode it.

   Pour the rest of the water on the foundation and watch the castle collapse.

Discuss this question: "What can we do to cement the foundation instead of erode it?"

3. According to the Gallup Youth Survey, the need to be trusted is the biggest need for teenagers. Work on strengthening trust with an exercise they may have done before: the Trust Fall.

Stand closely behind your teenager and ask him or her to stand straight with locked knees—like a solid board. With arms folded across the chest, he or she falls into your arms. The first time, catch your teen after about a foot. Repeat the process several times, increasing the distance to 18 inches, then 2 feet. Have them try falling back with closed eyes. Make sure you catch your teen each time. Don't even pretend to drop them. (You're next!) Switch places.

Discuss questions like these:

- How might a teen fall and ruin the trust she has with her parents?

- How might a teen strengthen his parents' trust?

Now try the Trust Fall in front of a full-length mirror, so your teen can see you behind him. Make a comment like this: "When we have truth, we can have trust. You can see me in the mirror, so you know what's true. You *know* I'm behind you and will catch you."

Ask your teen two additional questions:

- Can you trust me more when you can see me?

- What might the mirror represent in our relationship? (Honest and current communication.)

4. In an observant Jewish home you will find a small plaque, a mezuzah, by the front door with Scripture on it. Decide

on a positive saying with your teenager to post by the door of your home. For instance, "Trust = Truth Applied to Relationship." Make your mezuzah out of paper, wood, ceramics, or other material. Use it as a reminder to encourage each other.

5. Play Hot Seat. Buy something hot to eat or drink such as coffee latte, Hot Tamales candy, or spicy Mexican food. Ask your teen one question that will put him or her on the hot seat—but that won't get them in trouble. A sample question is, "Why aren't you friends with Terry anymore?" After the question is answered, give your teen some hot food or drink as a reward. Then it's your turn to be on the hot seat; your teen gets to ask you a question. Whatever you learn is confidential and may not be used against the teen for discipline.

TOOLS TO USE AT CHURCH

1. Take your own survey of parents and teens at your church. Ask teens what they want most in their parents. Ask parents what they want most in their teens. Ask for at least five qualities. Let parents and teens discuss the results together.

2. Buy Play-Doh or borrow it from the children's ministry. Remind parents and teens, "Parenting isn't sculpting; it's management. Good parenting does not guarantee a good outcome." Have the teens fashion the perfect parent while parents create the perfect teen. Discuss the qualities sculpted into the masterpieces.

3. Play *Generation Gap* based on a TV game show such as *Jeopardy*. Contrast the parent generation with the teen generation. Ask questions about music, culture, TV, world events, food, and other topics representative of each generation.

4. Show highlights of World Wrestling Federation bouts recorded from TV. Offer a fun, tension-releasing water balloon fight. Or you might want to use Batacca bats—short, foam-covered bats available at toy and sport stores—or paint guns. Use safety equipment when appropriate. Team up in combinations such as dads and daughters against mothers and sons. Make the last round parents against teens.

5. Choose an idea from the list below (Trust-Building Ideas for Parents and Teens) to do with other parents and teens. When the activity is finished, meet for snacks. Play a video of an old TV show (*Andy Griffith* or *The Cosby Show*) in the background to set the mood for trust!

Trust-Building Ideas for Parents and Teens

To increase the likelihood of having *quality* time, you need to have *quantity* time with your teen. Teens think, *I spend time with those I trust.* Enhance the level of parent-teen trust in your relationship with the following ideas:

- Go bowling, but bowl with your weak hand.

- Pick a place on the map (within twenty miles) that you have never been to and enjoy a drive together. Explore the town when you get there.

- Make a *Poser* Poster, incorporating people who pose as big shots—or who are treated like big shots—but who do not live up to ethical standards.

- Hike up a hill at night. Write the words to Matthew 5:14-16 on an index card. Bring it and a flashlight with you. Discuss what it means to be a light on the hill.

- Go out to eat at a nice restaurant. After dinner, ask the server to bring the dessert tray, spend a minute talking and looking but don't order anything. Then discuss resisting temptation.

⁜ Go to a music store and use the headphones to listen to each other's three favorite new CDs.

⁜ Get out your high school yearbook and take a short trip down memory lane with your teen. Share stories about your favorite and least favorite teachers. Compare the fashions then and now.

⁜ Visit a cemetery. Bring a Bible with you so you can discuss 1 Corinthians 15:35-37 with your teen. Share answers to this question: "What difference does Jesus make?"

⁜ Watch a TV show popular with teens, paper in hand. Draw a line down the middle. On one side, list references or scenes that are positive about Christianity or Christian values. In the other column, list the ones that go against these. (Or you can simply make tic marks for each occurrence.) Then discuss the results.

⁜ Try a new hobby or sport together. If you don't know what to try, tour the hobby store or the sporting goods store and decide together.

There you have it, ten ideas to build trust with your teenager. Don't worry if your teen gives you grief. It's part of the routine. Deep down he is thinking, *My parent really likes me. I mean, they actually want to do something fun with me! They must love me.* At another level, he is thinking, *They must be flipping out! I think they blew a circuit. It must be their age. Why would I want to be seen in public with them?* But don't let that sidetrack you!

Persist. Stay the course.

Remember, *you* are the parent. When your teen gives you a hard time, respond with wisdom and maturity and whine, "You're not the boss of me!"

CHAPTER 2

A Cry for Love

We give him whatever he needs. He has nice clothes. We just bought him shoes; they cost over a hundred dollars." Tracy, a forty-something mom, gestured at her fifteen-year-old son's new Nikes. "He's involved in sports, the youth group here at church, and he has lots of friends—but something's missing."

"What's your view of it?" I directed my question to Rich, Connor's dad.

"Well, it seems that Connor has a self-esteem problem. I don't know why. We always cheer him on and try to say positive things to him. I've given him everything he wants. I do know something is wrong. I assume it might be with us. That's why we're here."

"I am glad that the three of you came in to talk. I think it will help. Anything else you can tell me?"

"I work," said Tracy, "but I still make it a priority to make sure he has food in the house and clean clothes to wear. I want him to know I love him, that's why I do these things." She looked across my office to Connor, who was staring at his shoelaces. She caught his eye.

Connor blushed and went back to staring at his feet.

"Connor, what's your take? Do they understand you?"

"No, they don't." He looked up. "They totally miss it. I don't have a self-esteem problem, Dad. I feel okay about me. I don't have to have stuff or a bunch of things done for me. I can take care of myself."

"Then what's the problem?" I asked him.

"The problem isn't me. It's *them!*"

I was surprised by the sudden rise of volume in his voice.

"Just as I thought," muttered Rich under his breath.

"This is just the kind of reaction we've been getting," explained Tracy.

"Rich, Tracy, do you love Connor?"

"Of course."

"Certainly."

"Do you *tell* him that you love him?"

"All the time."

Rich nodded in agreement with his wife.

"When was the last time you told your son that you love him?"

"A few days ago when I dropped him off at soccer practice."

"How about you, Rich?"

"It might have been a few weeks ago when he came in past curfew. I reminded him of the consequence, but I told him that I loved him."

"Connor, do your remember those times?"

"Yeah."

"Do they mean anything to you?"

He shrugged his shoulders.

"It's not exactly what you need?"

"No, not really."

"Do you feel loved by your parents?"

"Umm . . . ahh . . . no . . . I mean, I know they love me and everything, but I don't *feel* loved. It's like I'm a possession or a responsibility to them."

Rich raised his eyebrows and retreated back in his chair.

Tracy frowned and sighed.

"In spite of all of your attempts to express love, Connor doesn't feel loved by you. Does that surprise you?"

"It sure does! We tell him that we love him. We say encouraging things to him. We buy him nice things. We drive him everywhere and help him with all kinds of things, and he still doesn't feel loved?" Tracy asked. I could sense the hurt in her voice.

"What does he need to feel loved? I'm at a loss," admitted Rich, wrinkling his forehead.

"There are keys for love, and you have to use the right key to unlock his heart. That's why Connor doesn't feel loved. If you express love to him but use the wrong key, it doesn't open up his heart. You can't get in and bring the light of your love to him. You could try with great effort to break in, but unless you have the key that fits, you won't succeed."

Connor looked up, smiled at me, then turned to his parents and nodded.

I was encouraged by his affirmation. "The seven keys for love are based on my research on the Seven Cries of teens. Each cry is an expression of love in some way. There are seven cries and seven ways to respond in love. My guess is that you haven't been using Connor's key for love."

"What can we do? I mean, I thought I was doing the right thing," said Tracy.

"It's not a question of right versus wrong. It's what works, what makes a person feel loved. For instance, we tend to express love in the way *we* want to receive it. My guess is that your key to love is support. You probably feel loved when someone serves you in a way that makes you feel supported. Am I right, Tracy?"

"Exactly."

"Rich, my guess is that you really feel loved when someone encourages you by listening and responding with kind words."

"That's it."

"Connor, I know that your parents love you. There's no doubt in my mind. They just need to figure out a way to express it in a way that feels like love to you. I would guess that your love key is different from your mom's and dad's. Would you feel loved by your parents if they would spend focused time with you, uninterrupted by their cell phones, TV, or other distractions? Or does love feel like a hug to you or just being close to each other?"

"Yeah . . . I guess my love key is a blend of the two. I'm a physical guy. I'm into sports and like to work out. Hangin' with someone means they're important. Being close to them because you want to, not because you have to. I would like it if my parents had more time to be with me, maybe find something we could do together, just for fun."

"So when your parents do things for you or say encouraging words or give you a gift, it doesn't make you feel loved—at least, not as much as a hug or spending time with you."

"Yeah, probably. I would feel loved if they made time for me, real time. Not this hurried, get-in-my-face-for-three-minutes intense stuff. Just the relaxing, chilling out you can do with a good friend. You know, being with each other doesn't mean you have to have 'a point.'"

"Rich, do you think you could schedule weekly one-on-one time with Connor for the next three weeks?"

"Sure, but I thought teens didn't want to be with their parents."

"It's all about time and place. You need to be careful when and where you're together. Make sure Connor has a say about it, but our research indicates that teens would like to spend *more* time with their parents, not less."

"So, my son is going to feel loved if I spend more time with him? And some of these problems . . . what do we do about them?"

"If a teen feels loved, most of the problems take care of themselves. If he doesn't feel loved, the problems become significant. The key to teens is to use their key of love to unlock their hearts. For example, Connor might like a hug from you."

Rich shifted in his seat, "Well, I . . . uhh . . . I'm not sure I'm comfortable with that. After all, he's fifteen; he's practically a man."

"We aren't talking about *your* comfort. We're talking about how to make your son feel loved. Sometimes it will be uncomfortable. Expressing love is a choice. It isn't simply an expression of a feeling."

"Okay, sure." Awkwardly, he got up and moved toward his son. He gave him a stiff side-hug and then returned to his seat.

"Connor, what did that feel like to you?"

"Weird, but I like it."

"What did it feel like?"

"Well, it felt like love—it made me feel loved."

Rich looked at me dejectedly and sighed, "I wish I would have known this earlier. He seemed so closed off to us."

"Using the right key opens his heart. Try to find new ways of expressing your love to Connor through his *love key*. Give him a high five, slap him on the back, give him a shoulder rub, wrestle with him. Teens need loving touches the most during the time in their lives when most parents back off. We reason that they're too old for it. But when you touch your teen like you did when he was a kid, it helps him feel secure and loved. Now your challenge for the week will be to discover ways you can express love to Connor in his keys of time and touch. I believe that as he feels loved, most of these peripheral issues will take care of themselves."

A Universal Need

When we polled teens with the Gallup Youth Survey, we asked them to tell us how strong certain needs were in their lives. Ninety-three percent said "the need to be understood and loved" was an important one, which means that it is the second-highest cry, according to our survey. The only need that scored higher, the need to be trusted, was just half a percent higher.[1] The distinction is practically irrelevant. It is safe to say that our teens want to be trusted *and* loved.

Like Connor's parents, sometimes we are at a loss about how to love our teens. How can we love our teens in ways that make them feel loved?

The Seven Love Keys of Teenagers

One of the primary sources of conflict between parents and teenagers comes from the parents continuing to parent their teens the same way they did when the kids were younger. But teenagers are not children. They are on the path toward adulthood. One of their goals is to pursue their independence and identity. I joke with parents of teenagers by telling them, "Your teen has one main goal in her pursuit to discover who she is: *to not be you.*"

When we can affirm our teens' uniqueness by loving them with their own love keys, we accomplish two things: loving them in ways that feel like love to them, and affirming and accepting their identities apart from us. To not do this is a set-up for conflict.

Nine out of ten of our teens feel love is a prominent need in their lives. A lot of teens feel alone, in the dark, and unloved. When we use their own love keys to open their hearts' doors, we let in the light and comfort that they need. It's like they are solar powered and need a recharge of fresh sunlight. With the right key, we can unlock their hearts and recharge their solar love cells.

Everyday life drains our heart's solar cells. We need a regular recharge of love coming from outside of ourselves. Without the opening of the heart's door with the right key of love, the heart becomes closed, dark, and cold. One of the loudest cries from our teens is the cry for love. From the chart on the next page, consider how the Seven Cries relate to the seven love keys.

The Seven Love Keys of Teens

Cries	Love Keys	Key Words
for trust	time	being there, connecting
for love	commitment	promise, devotion
for security	touch	physical closeness and presence
for purpose	mission	direction, guidance, destiny
to be heard	words	encouraging and affirming words
to be valued	gifts	honor, thoughtfulness
for support	support	service, help

Using the seven love keys can affirm your teen's uniqueness and make your teen feel loved. Let's consider them one by one.

LOVE KEY 1: TIME

Trust is the first cry of teens, and part of that cry is the call for parents and adults to be there for teenagers. It takes time to build trust. Trust cannot be produced at microwave speed. Trust is organic; it grows as we invest valuable deposits of time into the relationship. Focused time means giving your teenager your undivided attention. During the moments you are together, nothing else matters. Time communicates love to the teen with this key to trust.

In our media-soaked age of information, we can place an over-inflated value on words. Messages bombard us from all angles—TV, the Internet, newspapers, magazines, telephone, radio, junk mail, and personal digital assistants. It is easy to think that the verbal world is the most important. But that isn't necessarily so. Sometimes we can send a powerful message, a message of love, by just spending time with someone. Not filling it with intense conversation, but just logging the time together.

Don't believe in the myth of quality time when it comes to your teenager. You cannot say, "I have thirty minutes. Let's get into an intense conversation before I have to go." With teens it usually does not happen that way. To get some quality time you have to have chunks of quantity time. It's as though you need to have "junk time" to refine like dross to get the gold of quality time.

When teens sense that you are including them into a block of time, they are more likely to open up. For instance, have you noticed how open they are to talk while you are in the car on a long drive? They feel safe. The car is a great equalizer. They don't feel overpowered by the parent's authority or communication skills. At any given moment, the teen can say, "Hey, look at that!" There is an automatic escape for the teen while riding in the car with mom or dad.

This is what I mean by "quality comes with quantity." You need to plant some seemingly wasted minutes to harvest a few special moments. You will know you are doing this when your teen drones on and on, then drops a gem: "Well, then we went to the mall, but nothing much was happening there except a sale at Old Navy, and I found the cutest top, but they didn't have my size. Anyway, we went to this party at Melissa's house. You remember her sister? She was a cheerleader a few years ago. She—I mean, Melissa—lives down by 7-Eleven. Her sister is in college now, but anyway, some guys who usually hang out and smoke at 7-Eleven heard about the party at Melissa's and crashed it. I mean, nobody knows them, but they just showed up. And you wouldn't believe what happened . . ."

Got your attention? You have to put up with a lot of oysters to get a few pearls.

The way my friend John Trent describes it, being there is about going beyond casual acquaintances to make deep, lasting connections. To be there for someone adds a sense of mission and purpose to our lives, even as it subtracts fear and isolation. It helps us focus our days and maintain wonder as we age. To be there is to be emotionally and spiritually in the present moment for your children, your spouse, and yourself.[2]

Being there with our teenagers mean spending time with them. When we make the effort to be there for our teens, we send messages that they are important to us. It helps them feel connected, on course, and not so alone in uncharted territory. When we invest time with our teenager, we are increasing the trust level. A cry for trust is often a cry for love. "Do you love me enough to entrust me with some of your time?"

LOVE KEY 2: COMMITMENT

The second-highest response in our survey was the cry for love, which we respond to with the love key of commitment.

When we speak of *love* in a world where many teens have experienced divorce, they might respond, "That's what my parents had before things got bad and they split up." But this doesn't make millennials jaded and cynical. Most are looking forward to a successful, long-term marriage. In a fast-paced, ever-changing, increasingly technological world, there is something soothing and comforting about a simple promise kept. For some teens, their love key is when we keep our promises, making a commitment to them and sticking to it.

For girls, this may be seen as meeting their emotional need for stability and consistency. "If someone loves and understands me, he will make a commitment to be with me." Commitment, a traditional value, is prevalent among today's teens, who are desperately seeking reliability and constancy.

Love is a promise kept—a vow held dear, protected, and upheld. You might say that teens with this love key are from Missouri, which is known as "The Show Me State." Teens with the love key of commitment want to see love in action in the form of a promise kept. Words, gifts, time, mission, and touch do not mean that much to these teens. They are looking for devotion.

The love key can easily be seen in the massive chastity rallies where thousands of teens make a stand for abstinence. Millions of teens have completed a pledge to remain virgins until they are married. Most are doing this as an expression of their Christian faith that teaches sex is reserved for married couples. Some proudly wear rings or necklaces, which symbolize their commitment to purity. In recent years, we have seen nationally known teenage celebrities declare their stands for abstinence and point to their rings or their cross necklaces signifying their commitment. Consider providing a commitment ceremony for your teen, complete with jewelry and written pledges.

A smaller step might be to evaluate the promises that you have made to your teen. Write them down and give yourself a grade on how well you have kept them. If you have C's or lower, ask yourself, "What gets in the way of keeping my promises to my teen?" Express to your teen your desire to be a promise-keeping parent. Ask him or her, "What are the top two or three promises that you would like me to keep as an evidence of my love for you?"

Sometimes the cry for love is simply a cry for living up to our promises.

LOVE KEY 3: TOUCH

The third cry of today's teenager is a cry for security. This is a cry for physical and emotional safety. For girls, safety is especially important, with 85 percent reporting that "to feel safe and secure where I live and go to school" is a "very strong" need.

When a teen has had a confusing day at school and a friend has said something hurtful, a parent's words may or may not help, but sometimes an appropriate touch can do wonders. When we reflect on our teens' preschool years, we draw up memories of cuddling with our kids, reading to them as we twist their hair, wrestling with them, and pushing them on the swing. Each of these memories involves touching. Touch can be an effective means of recharging the hearts of our teens.

I have observed that many parents touch their teens less than they did in the elementary years. This is disappointing because I believe appropriate touch is needed *more* in the teen years, not less. Granted, you can't hug your 240-pound lineman son and give him a kiss as you drop him off in front of the high school, but you can give him a pat on the shoulder as you drive, before you enter the school parents-don't-touch zone (which is about the same as the tobacco-free zone at most high schools).

"Remember time and place," I caution parents. When you express affection to your teenager, make sure it is the right time and the right place. If you are not sure, ask your teenager. Teenagers generally do not like much touching in public, but they might be more open to it in the privacy of your home. Make sure they don't have friends over when you plant big smooches on their cheeks. This can be embarrassing for most teens.

When I was a youth pastor, I made it my habit to memorize the names of the teens in my youth group, greet them by name, and touch them in some appropriate way every week. For most it was a modified handshake, a high five, or a touch on the shoulder as they passed by. For some, it was a quick hug or pat on the back—whatever they were most comfortable with. Did you catch that? Whatever *they* were most comfortable with. It took me a while, but I eventually knew the comfort level of each student who regularly came to our group, and I made the appropriate physical contact with them.

Years later, I was talking with some of our graduates who had become young adults. I asked, "What was it that you remember about our youth group?"

"It was your greeting, your calling me by name, and your handshake."

"Your high five and you knowing my name was the highlight for me."

"Tim, your hugs were the only ones I ever got. My parents never hugged me. I remember those more than your talks."

"I can't believe you memorized hundreds of our names and took the time each week to greet each of us and do our goofy seven-point handshake. I know you worked hard on your lessons and everything, but that handshake and your smile made me feel loved."

The Gallup Youth Survey reports that three out of four teens believe that fathers should hug their teenagers at least once a week. Fifty-five percent of the same teens reported that their own fathers do give them a hug at least once a week.

Be encouraged! Most teens want a hug and think they are getting what they need. Don't be afraid to reach out and tickle your teen!

LOVE KEY 4: MISSION

The fourth cry of teens is "to believe that life is meaningful and has a purpose." If we consider the teens who responded to this issue as a "very strong need," it would be only one percentage point off of the highest-scoring needs of trust, love, and security. Seventy-seven percent of the teens surveyed reported that believing "life is meaningful and has a purpose" is a "very strong" need. An additional 14.5 percent reported it as a "strong need," giving us a total of 91.5 percent of the teens indicating that this is essential in their lives. In other words, having a purpose in life is very important to millennials. They are on a mission to pursue meaning.

Millennials are desperately in search of heroes. Many are unlikely to find one, so they will attempt to become one. Because of the obvious absence of positive role models for young people, millennials will answer the call to heroism and emerge as the next generation of heroes.

As we take a closer look at today's teens, we can observe seeds of heroism:

- Today's teens have a great concern for the decline in moral and social values.

- They want to see leaders with strong moral character.

- Fewer are sexually active. Many are committed to abstinence.

❖ Fewer of today's teens drink beer, their first-choice drug.

❖ Volunteerism is on the rise.

❖ Most are committed to moving beyond their parents' views of race and affirm diversity.[3]

Millennials could be pegged as neotraditionalists. They like some of the old-fashioned values of their grandparents and the strong archetypal heroes from the G. I. Generation such as John F. Kennedy, John Wayne, and Ronald Reagan. They are attracted to leaders with a strong sense of purpose. Their cry is for purpose, and their love key is to be offered a mission that is beyond them. Love, to them, is being involved in a worthy cause.

This can be particularly confusing to boomer parents who do not understand the cry for purpose. Success to many boomers means looking young and successful and achieving. They cannot comprehend their teenage sons and daughters whose key to love is a "sense of destiny in my life." But understanding them is critical. Many boomer parents may marginalize their teen's key to love because it is difficult to understand and support it. When we can reach beyond our comfort zone and express love to our teens in ways that open their hearts, we are using the correct key to love.

In the discussion of love, it is vital to be guiding our teens with a sense of destiny. Christian parents can use the concept of living according to our God-given design. God has created us in such a way that, when we live according to His unique design for us, we live effective lives, enjoy ourselves, and please God.

One way we can help express love to teens with this key is to become mentors or to provide mentors for them. I define mentoring as *a connection between youth and a caring adult from whom they can learn and receive coaching, encouragement, support, and guidance.* All teens are seeking direction, but those with mission as their key to love desperately need someone to help clarify their purpose and point them in the direction of their God-given destiny. To these teens, mission is love.

LOVE KEY 5: WORDS

The fifth cry of today's teen is to be heard. Teens want a voice. They want to be heard above the noise. When we listen to our teens, we show them that they are important, that their words are worth listening to. We show worth to a person by paying attention to what they say. We can also demonstrate love and worth by the words we say to our teenagers. Adolescence is the stage of life that needs affirming words the most. Teens are struggling with competency, identity, acceptance, and comparison. Adolescence is an emotionally trying time. A word of affirmation can make the difference in the life of your teenager.

One way to affirm your teen is with words of praise. Look for ways to recognize your teen's accomplishments and commend her. Make sure you are sincere and specific. It is better to say, "I like the way you prepare to baby-sit by thinking of games and activities to do with the children," than, "You are a good baby-sitter."

When we are specific, we are affirming and guiding. We are always looking for ways to guide and influence teenagers without receiving reactions from them. One of the proven ways is to guide with specific words of praise.

Our daughter Brooke plays on her high school basketball team. At a recent game, they were beaten by a crosstown rival. I tried to encourage her after the game as we walked to the car.

"I'm sorry you didn't win."

"We should have."

"Yeah, I know. But I thought you played well; you were all over the court. You had ten rebounds."

"Oh, really? I didn't know I had that many. I never count. I just play."

"Your rebounds kept us in play. It gave us a chance to shoot."

"Our shooting was terrible."

"You're right. Your team usually shoots better. But you can't always influence that. I can't believe how high you jumped to out-rebound that tall girl on the other team."

A broad smile splashed across her face, "Yeah, that was fun!"

Sometimes our teens win. Sometimes they lose. We can't always affirm results. In either situation, we can affirm their efforts and their progress. When we do not affirm effort and progress, we set up an atmosphere of perfectionism. If we only express words of praise when our teens succeed (the end result), we rob them of what they can learn through the *process*. We become product-oriented, rather than process-oriented.

Some parents become focused on their teens' failure to reach the end product. All the parents see is failure. They cannot see the effort. Because they are focused on success, they can't affirm their teens for trying. When these teens need an encouraging word from Mom or Dad, they don't receive one—because they didn't live up to their parents' expectations. Instead of offering words of praise, these product-oriented parents offer criticism or negative comments. This can be destructive to teens, especially those with the love key of words. A teen might be thinking, *The reason I tried out for orchestra was because of my parents' encouragement. Now, when I don't make first chair, they're all critical. I can never measure up. Why can't they be excited that I'm playing better and that I made second chair? Why do I always have to be perfect?*

Praise the process. Praise any progress. Celebrate any movement in the right direction. I have noticed that teens respond to these kinds of encouraging words.

Words of affection are another way to express love. Praise focuses on the behavior and progress of the teenager, but words of affection focus on the teenager himself. *I love you* is a common phrase that expresses affection. But sometimes it sounds awkward when you are directing it toward your teenager. Let's admit it: It's easier to say it to an adoring three-year-old than a gangly, pimply-faced thirteen-year-old who keeps borrowing your clothes without permission.

Many teens have fathers who tell their children that they love them at least once a week. According to the Gallup Youth Survey, 66 percent of the teens surveyed said that their fathers definitely tell their teens they love them at least once a week.[4] This is encouraging and powerful. But what about the other 34 percent who go weeks or months or years without a word of affection from their dads or moms? These are the teens who are likely to feel unloved.

You may not be comfortable saying *I love you* to your teenager. Try these alternatives:

- I'm proud of you.

- I like the way you handled yourself in that situation.

- I enjoyed our time together.

- You're a fun person to be with.

- I can see you've really been doing some thinking.

- If I could choose any kid in the world, I'd choose you.

Have you noticed that sometimes teens discount the words *I love you* anyway? They reason, *Of course you love me. You have to. You're my parent. It's your job to love me.* One way to express love to your teen with words of affirmation is to use a word picture. Instead of coming right out and saying, "I love you," you can try a side-door approach—one that is not so direct. It sneaks up on them. I guess you could call it *stealth affirmation.*

A word picture is an analogy that you can use to express words of affirmation to your teenager. It is a picture that parallels the words of affirmation that you want to give your teen. Let me give you some examples.

✢ "Before I saw the kitchen, I was worn out from work and felt like a sailboat stalled on the sea without any wind in sight. When you cleaned up the kitchen without being told, it made me feel like a sailboat with a powerful breeze filling the sails. Thanks. Your thoughtfulness has really perked me up."

✢ "I noticed that you took time to play ball with the neighbor kid. I know he can be whiny and pesky. He probably comes home every day from school wishing that his dad still lived there. I bet he feels like an NBA superstar when he beats you at Horse. You're very generous with your time when you play basketball with him."

Simple comparisons sometimes have more impact than direct compliments. A word picture, offered in love, opens up the heart of a teenager who might be closed to other expressions of love.

Another way to use the love key of words is by asking for your teen's opinion. Remember, the cry to be heard relates to this love key. Teens want a voice. They want to express their opinions and values. Give them a forum to do this. I am convinced that some teens don't feel loved unless they have the opportunity to share their views. To them, love equals a listening audience. They do not feel loved unless they have one or more people who are willing to listen to them and dialogue with them about important issues.

To experiment with this, pick a topic from the headlines and ask your teen at the dinner table to share his opinion on it. Be ready for some lively conversation and possibly some controversy.

LOVE KEY 6: GIFTS

The sixth cry of teens is to be valued. Sixty-eight percent of the teens surveyed reported a "very strong need" to "be appreciated or valued." Another 21 percent rated it as a "strong need," for a total of 89 percent of teens reporting they want to be valued.

By giving gifts we can use a love key to express personal value. For some teens, an inexpensive but thoughtful gift may make them feel loved—more than any other love key. It is the key that fits the doors to their hearts. All teens are not verbal or expressive. They may be more comfortable with nonverbal expressions of affection.

I am part of the Heritage Builder movement, dads and moms who take seriously their responsibility to build a family of faith. In our research we have discovered that one of the key ways to make an impact on a child is to give him a special gift to commemorate a rite of passage. Millions of parents have given their sons and daughters gold rings as their teens have made vows to save sex for marriage. Others have discovered the power of a tradition like a Christian Bar or Bat Mitzvah that is similar to the Jewish rite of passage that acknowledges the young person's commitment to faith and the faith community. A gold or silver cross and a leather-bound Bible are appropriate gifts for these events. Other families have a rite of passage upon high school graduation and might give their sons a sword or their daughters a pendant, to signify their worth and entrance into adulthood.[5]

Each of these special events takes on more significance when gifts are involved. For some teens, their love key is giving and receiving gifts. They feel loved when they receive a gift. They enjoy expressing their love through the giving of gifts.

For some, this love key is the most difficult; it requires an investment and, at times, sacrifice. Parents of teens with this love key will need to study them to see what kinds of gifts are meaningful. This insight is part of the gift. Teens with gifts as their love key feel valued when someone takes the time to know what they would like and then makes the effort to obtain it and present it.

My wife, Suzanne, has the love key of gifts. We were married almost twenty years before I realized it. I wish I would have known earlier. For years, I expressed love to her in the way I wanted to be loved, through *my* love keys of words and support. I would say loving things to her and make sacrifices for her, but they did not seem to impact her. I knew she appreciated them, but they didn't mean *love* to her.

Now I know. Love to her is spelled G-I-F-T.

I struggled with this because words and deeds are cheap, and gifts cost me money. Especially since her love key works the best when it comes in the form of jewelry.

You may have experienced something similar. You have been trying to express your love through words, time, promises, touch, or acts of support, but they don't seem to get through to your teenager's heart. Try a gift. Study your teen to see what she likes, then, without notice or any strings attached, give her a gift.

You might ask yourself, "When was the last time I gave a gift to my teenager with no strings attached?" Did you require anything from your teen before or after you gave the gift? If so, that wasn't a gift.

As I reflect, I like to give gifts to my wife because I love her, not because I am trying to influence her, change her, or manipulate her. I give because I love. I need to do the same with my teen.

Some parents do not know their own teen's love key and have not taken the time to discover it; as a result, they find it convenient to buy them things instead of spending time with them or making the effort to discover what unlocks their heart. This only works in for the short term. Teens are quick to discern when parents are trying to buy love. That is not what this discussion about gifts is about. A gift is a symbol of our love, not a replacement for it.

LOVE KEY 7: SUPPORT

The seventh cry of teens is the need to be supported in their efforts. For some teens, their key of love is not what you say or give but what you *do* that makes the difference. These teens are looking for support as a sign of love for them. For some teenagers, words, touch, and time are appreciated, but these love keys don't *feel* like love to them. If you mention acts of support you provided during their lifetime, they may say, "Yeah, that feels like love to me." These teens have the love key of support. They feel especially loved when parents take the time to support them in their efforts and activities:

- Picking them up from school

- Taking them shopping

- Doing their laundry

- Grocery shopping for them

- Cooking meals for them

- Taking them to their music lessons

- Baking cookies for their sports team

- Volunteering to be the team mom

- Staying up late and helping with school projects

- Picking them and their band mates up—after the away game at one A.M.

These are just a few ways parents of teens show love through support. It's easy to overlook them. Because we constantly serve our children, it's easy to forget that the daily and routine tasks we perform are actually expressions of love to our teens. Your kids may forget the words you expressed, but they may retain for years the memory of a supportive act you offered.

Rosalyn was in my office for counsel about her fifteen-year-old son, Jake. "He seems so defiant, and I've tried everything to get to him."

I mentioned the seven love keys and asked, "Do you think he would respond to your words of affirmation or commitment?"

"No."

"How about quality time or touch?"

She shook her head sideways.

"How about support?"

Her eyebrow rose. A smile slowly crept across her face, "Yes, maybe that's it. I don't know. I've tried everything. I've tried speaking kind and affirming words, but it's like water off a duck's back. I've spent time with him doing exactly what he wants to do for a whole Saturday. I even tried showing more affection, but that was a disaster. So, why not? I'm willing to try."

"What is his least favorite chore?"

"Oh, that's easy. Every Saturday he has to clean his room. He can't go out until it's done. He usually sleeps in until eleven, then I spend two hours cajoling him to do it. It only takes him about an hour, but it's a hassle."

"Does he go out on Fridays?"

"Most of the time."

"Okay, this Friday night, you clean his room. Do it just the way you like it. In other words, really clean it instead of piling everything in his closet. Then leave a note with a great big red heart on it that says, 'I cleaned your room for you, because I love you. Enjoy sleeping in.'"

"Isn't that a bribe?"

"No. You aren't asking him to do anything."

"Isn't it irresponsible?"

"No. You're only doing it once, not every week."

"Why would I do this?"

"To demonstrate love to him in his love key."

Rosalyn did what I suggested, then called me the following Monday. "Guess what happened when Jake woke up?"

"He immediately started messing up his room?"

"Well, yeah, that's right. But he came down and thanked me. He said, 'Thanks, Mom, for cleaning my room.' He walked over to the kitchen table where I was drinking coffee and reading the paper, and he gave me a hug. He actually bent over, kissed the top of my head, and said, 'Mom, I love you.' I nearly fell out of the chair!"

"That's great. I guess his love key is support."

"I agree. But then reality crashed in. As soon as he said, 'I love you,' he asked me, 'What's for breakfast?' I guess some things never change."

Loving the Obnoxious

Sometimes teens are annoying and obnoxious. We simply don't *feel* like loving them. How are we to love our teens when they seem so unlovely?

Whether it's loving our teenagers in ways that they understand or loving them when we don't feel like it, both situations require resources beyond our own. We do not always have the strength to express love the way our teens receive it. We do not always have the fortitude or patience to love them when they are acting like three-year-olds.

How do we love the obnoxious?

Ask your Father—your heavenly Father—to help you. He does the same thing for us. I am sure there are times when God looks at us and thinks, *Are they doing that again? I thought they would have grown past that.*

But He doesn't zap us from heaven with a lightning bolt. He is patient and kind. His mercy is deep. He gives us another chance.

> Remember, O LORD, your great mercy and love, for they are from of old. Remember not the sins of my youth and my rebellious ways; according to your love remember me, for you are good, O LORD. (Psalm 25:6-7 NIV)

We usually hear 1 Corinthians, the Love Chapter, read at weddings, but the truths found there are guidance for showing love to our teens. The following is my paraphrase of 1 Corinthians 13 for parents of teens:

Love for Your Teenager

Love is patient—even when they roll their eyes back
  to the top of their heads.
Love is kind—especially when you feel like being mean.
Love does not envy their energy.
Love does not boast about the good ol' days.
Love is not proud of all your adult accomplishments.
Love is not rude, even when it is one A.M. and
  the stereo is blasting.
Love is not self-seeking, even though they act like
  life is all about them.
Love is not easily angered. Save it for the really big issues.
Love keeps no record of wrongs. Forgiveness is like
  a mental eraser.
Love does not delight in evil but rejoices with the truth.
  Integrity and authenticity are pursued, not perfection.
Love always protects, even when they try to
  pull away from our care.
Love always trusts. We believe them until we have
  proof that we should not.
Love always hopes. We expect the best from our teens.
Love always perseveres. We keep trying.
Love never fails. The impact in living is loving.

Discussion Questions

PARENT TO PARENT

1. Look back at the scenario that opens this chapter. Who do you most closely identify with: Connor (teen), Rich (dad), or Tracy (mom)? Why?

2. Do you think some parents of teens will be shocked to discover their teens' love key? Explain your thoughts.

3. How can the seven love keys be used to affirm your teen's uniqueness?

4. Do you agree that "one of the primary sources of conflict between parents and teenagers comes from parents trying to parent the same way they did when their teens were younger"? Discuss your answers.

5. How might you use the seven love keys with your teen?

TALKING WITH YOUR TEEN

1. Share the seven love keys with your teen. Describe which key is yours. How do you know?

2. Ask your teen: "Which one of the love keys means love to you?" Encourage him to explain and give examples.

3. Ask your teen: "Which one of the love keys is the least effective for you?" Discuss her answer.

4. Discuss this question with your teen: "When you think of your friends, which love key is the most common?"

5. Have your teen describe three ways you could show love to him in his love key.

Responding to the Cry

THE CRY

The cry for love.

THE CHALLENGE

To express our love in ways that make our teens feel loved by us, rather than in ways we prefer to express love.

TOOLS TO USE AT HOME

1. Work through the seven love keys material in this chapter and determine your love key. Write a list of five ways you feel loved based on your love key and share it with your family.

2. Write an e-mail or a note to your teen offering praise and affection.

3. Once a day, hug your teenager. If your teen is prone to squirm out of it, sneak up behind him before you serve dinner and say, "No dinner until you hug the cook."

4. Use your calendar to schedule one-on-one time with your teen at least once a week for the next four weeks.

5. Review the supportive acts you can offer that are listed on page 66. Choose one to do this week for your teen. Let her know you did it because you love her. "I drive you to all of your activities because I love you."

TOOLS TO USE AT CHURCH

1. Discuss with the youth pastor the idea of offering ceremonial gifts (a Bible, a cross, religious art, concordance, etc.) at key rites of passage like confirmation, graduation from middle or

high school, or baptism. Work with other parents to raise the money and provide a meaningful service at these important times.

2. Develop a purity-pledge rite to encourage teens to remain sexually pure until marriage. Coordinate a celebration of chastity with the pastor or youth pastor, including gifts, vows, mementos, photos, and music.

3. Design a Big Brother/Big Sister program for the youth group that pairs up new freshmen with a mature, Christian junior or senior. Ask the big brothers and big sisters to call their younger siblings in the program, get to know them, and include them in the youth group activities. Design a fun activity just for those in the program. Ask adults in the church to help fund some of these events or to bring food. Let the adults know their contributions are a way of showing love—from the contributors to the older students who pass it on to the younger students.

4. At least twice a year, design a service project for the youth group that provides opportunities for teens to express love by helping other people. This could be anything from a car wash to raising money for camp scholarships to helping the elderly with their home maintenance.

5. Have a parent pride banquet where the teens cook, serve, and entertain their parents. Make it special by having the kids dress up and by serving sparkling cider in plastic champagne glasses. Use tablecloths and candlelight. Have students play soft instrumental music on a piano or stringed instruments. Have a student emcee and a few other students share words of affirmation for their parents. Provide a time for students to sit next to their parents and read them a tribute that they have written. This banquet is a profound way to honor parents.

CHAPTER 3

A Cry for Security

Today's teens are crying for security. They want to feel safe at school, at home, and in their communities. Because of the terrorist attacks and the school shootings, teens are now asking, *Where can I be safe?*

In our Gallup "Cries of Teens" Survey, we discovered that 92.1 percent of teens feel that security is "very important" or "important" to them. This is remarkably higher than polls prior to Columbine and September 11, 2001. It is only .1 percent lower than the second-place cry for love. Safety used to be assumed in our country—for children, teens, and adults. But it isn't now. We have lost the innocence of security; we are now a nation on edge. Our teens are crying for trust and love, but they are also crying for security. They want to be safe and live long enough to be loved and trusted.

The cry for security is considered a basic need—more basic than having a purpose or a sense of belonging. If teens do not feel safe, they will not be able to develop the higher needs such as meaning and identity. If teens do not have a minimal level of emotional and physical safety in their communities, they are unlikely to be involved in making it better.

The cry for security is a need for predictability, safety, and protection, and the desire for normalcy and fortification from surprises. As much as teenagers complain about routine and boredom, they are desperately seeking continuity, which makes them feel safe. In a changing world with changing bodies, teens are looking for something stable.

We live in uncertain times. Eighty-seven percent of the adults surveyed in a CNN/Gallup poll taken shortly after the 9/11 attacks reported "September 11 is the most tragic event of my life." Shocking. Unexpected. On U.S. soil. It all adds up to the same question our teens are asking, "Where can I be safe?"

A few days after the September 11 terrorism, children were interviewed for an afternoon TV talk show. One of the boys reported that his parents told him, "Don't worry. You don't know anyone who was killed. Be happy." The ten-year-old continued, "It didn't help. I'm still afraid and sad."

What makes our children feel safe? What does not? We will deal with these questions in this chapter. Our challenge is to create a secure environment so our teens can mature at a healthy and natural pace.

Daddy's Home

Security at home has a lot to do with fathers. George Gallup Jr., has done extensive research on fathers. He says:

> Fortunately the populace seems to recognize fully the importance of fatherhood to a healthy society. One survey shows that 79 percent of Americans say father absence is the nation's most significant problem. In addition, no fewer than 85 percent of Americans say that "the number of children being born to single parents" is either a critical or serious problem. . . . Seven in ten Americans believe a child needs a home with *both* a father and a mother to grow up happily, yet four

in ten children are not so blessed. Wade Horn, president of the National Fatherhood Initiative, writes: "Every child deserves the love, support, and nurturance of a legally and morally responsible father, because fathers are different from mothers in important ways and the father-child bond is important to the healthy development of children."

The key predictor of crime is not education or income, according to one objective study, but whether or not a child lives with his biological father.[1]

One of the most effective ways to reduce crime and violence in our country would be to develop strategies to keep men in the home and active in their role as father. It is critical that we do so if we hope to restore security and stability in America's homes.

Columnist Michael McManus writes about the need: "The tragic result is that nearly four of ten children—24 million kids—do not live in homes with their fathers. . . . Such abandonment is unprecedented in any nation. Three-fourths of those children will live in poverty before 11. They are more likely to fail in school, engage in early sex, and have drug or alcohol problems. And 70 percent of juvenile felons have absent fathers."[2]

Too many teens do not have the skills necessary to navigate adolescence. They don't have the one weapon they need to confront the risks they encounter: solid values, rooted in religious faith. The primary source of these values is parents. Fathers are especially needed. Dads are more critical than ever because of the loss of key support systems: strong families, extended families, friendly neighborhoods, and a society with general agreement on core values. Because of the lack of these support systems, today's teens are at high risk.

Michael McManus cites a provocative quote from a report by the Carnegie Council on Adolescent Development: "All together, nearly half of American adolescents are at high or moderate risk of seriously damaging their life chances. The damage may be near-term, or it may be delayed, like a time bomb."[3]

These threatening conditions exist among families of all income levels and backgrounds, in cities, suburbs, and rural areas.

My children like it when I am home. My late-night ritual is to check all the windows and doors and turn out the lights. I have been doing this since they were born. When I travel, I am not there to perform this ritual. Our daughters have told me that they experience more anxiety when I am gone. They have to remember to close all the windows, lock the doors, and turn out the lights.

On a basic level, the father's presence means Daddy's home to provide stability, to provide safety, and to provide resources, all of which may not be there if Daddy is gone.

When I'm home, there is a higher level of purposefulness around bedtime.

"Daddy will tuck me in."

"Daddy will lock the doors and check the windows."

"Daddy will keep us safe."

"We'll have what we need because Daddy's home."

Personal Security

George Gallup Jr., analyzed his data and wrote:

> Surveys clearly show that most Americans place high importance on family and fatherhood. Those among us who have had the blessing of a loving father must reach out to the four in ten children in our society who come home each day from school to fatherless homes. In fact, each of us at this moment might well ask ourselves this question: *Is there a child out there somewhere who deserves the same blessings I received from a father and who needs someone to walk alongside*

> *him or her through the travails of youth? Shouldn't we all*
> *be mentors of one kind or another?* If we do not reach
> out to the fatherless children in our nation, we can
> count on confronting severe societal problems for
> years to come. More importantly, as people who have
> experienced the love of an earthly father, and the love
> of God of the universe, can we do less?[4]

I like what George Gallup Jr. says: "Shouldn't we all be mentors of one kind or another?"

Think of how much security we could bring to homes, especially fatherless homes, if every teen in our country had a mentor. Maybe Colin Powell is on to something with his drive to provide mentors. He writes: "Is it possible to fill the gap that a missing father leaves in a child's life? Not completely, but the gap can be narrowed. The presence of a caring adult mentor may be enough to help that child avoid the worst pitfalls that beset fatherless children."[5]

Security to Teens

Security means different things to different people. If you talk to adults, they may refer to money in the bank, their retirement portfolios, their investments, or the security systems that arm their homes. According to my dictionary, security includes the concepts of protection, peace, insurance, and self-confidence. If you talk with a teenager you will get a completely different view of security.

Teens are more apt to talk about stability, dependability, consistency, and reliability when they are thinking about security. Because they live in a world of constant turmoil, they crave stability. Their own bodies are changing on them. *What can I depend on?* is a recurring question in the minds of teens. We live in a tumultuous culture. Most of our teens have experienced divorce. Twenty-seven percent of children in America live with only one biological parent. Perhaps one of the most troubling developments in our divorce culture is shared custody. Forcing children to have two beds, two closets of toys, an alternating schedule, and tense moments of drop-off and pickup leaves them certain of one thing: they can't count on anything at all.[6]

Millennials need anchors. They need shelter from the changing tides of culture. They need sources of predictability and permanence in an environment that is fluid. They need to know what to expect. Security helps millennials cope with their world and helps them navigate the changes and challenges of adolescence. Without these anchors, teens can feel rejected. Some have complained to me that "they feel set up" by a culture that has high expectations from them but does not protect them. Without a sense of security, some teens recoil with violence.

Security at School

Seven fatal school shootings in less than two school years. It will go down in American history as one of the riskiest times to go to high school. Moses Lake, Washington; Pearl, Mississippi; West Paducah, Kentucky; Jonesboro, Arkansas; Springfield, Oregon; Littleton, Colorado; and Conyers, Georgia. Sadly, the list has continued on. The recurrent images of teenage boys shooting up their schools filled the airwaves and our minds. Their hostile acts have captured the attention of our country. What we see frightens us.

During a report on the Littleton tragedy, the normally unflappable Geraldo Rivera was perplexed and noticeably agitated. He talked of just returning from covering the Kosovo war and how cruel the ethnic cleansing seemed to him, but how senseless this "Littleton thing" was.

I was watching at my health club while I was working out on a machine. I could not believe what I saw: a TV news anchor without the answer. He admitted that the teen violence was more upsetting

Generally, today's teens are satisfied with their personal lives, expect to have a happy and successful future and live to a ripe-old age. Yet some wonder if they will make it. Many feel physically unsafe—on the street, in school, even in their own homes. It is no exaggeration to say that we are a society at risk of losing a generation.

—*Gallup Tuesday Briefing,* 30 July 2002, adapted

than the Kosovo mass murders. He sat there, staring directly into the camera, speechless, shaking his head. Finally he said, "I don't get it, folks. Usually I have something to say, but this one has got me." He looked down at his script, rubbed his forehead, looked into the camera, and sighed, "We'll take a break. Back in a minute with 'Live from Littleton.'"

I turned to the people working out beside me and said, "Now that's not something you see every day."

The man on the treadmill shook his head, "Geraldo's stumped." He seemed pleased.

The woman on my left had a different reaction. She looked frightened and perplexed. "What is happening to our kids?" she asked.

"They're much more violent and vulnerable," I offered.

Geraldo said it well: "This one has got me." It summed up what all of us were feeling—scared and confused.

Time magazine was honest enough to admit that the news media are afraid because they think they should have the answers.

We love to explain everything, have the story wrapped up in a box for the weekend. But this is one we cannot fit into a box. A survey by the Pew Charitable Trust found that the Littleton shooting is one of the most closely followed stories of the decade. It lingers in part because of our failure to account for what happened. And some people in the media are frightened that the media are to blame.[7]

I must admit, I was entertained to see a media mogul like Geraldo struggle with the issues. It made him seem more human to me. It removed him from that pedestal that celebrities and news anchors are set upon (or build for themselves).

In recent years we have seen a surge in teenage rage. The violence has escalated and become deadlier. The stakes of teenage hostility have been raised. Like Geraldo, we don't get it. Why are our teenagers killing?

Some would say the reason is the media. That's what *Time* magazine is afraid of. Does a magazine contribute to the violence by covering the violence? Does it provide fodder for the copycat?

Media and Security

USA Today reported on a survey taken by the National Institute on Media and the Family: "Eighty-one percent of parents of two- to seventeen-year-olds agree that they are concerned about the violence their kids see in movies or on TV." More than half of the 527 parents in the survey, conducted *before* the April 1999 Littleton massacre, say that their children are affected by violence they see in video games, in movies, or on TV. The study also showed a concrete relationship between a family's media habits and student performance in school. And it revealed that students who watch a lot of television do not perform as well academically.[8]

We are worried about the impact of violent media images on our kids with valid reason. Hundreds of copycat crimes swept the country after Columbine. Teenagers committed all of the crimes. According to a Gallup poll, 37 percent of thirteen- to seventeen-year-olds across the nation have heard of Columbine-style threats at their own schools, and 20 percent said their schools had been evacuated because of a bomb threat.[9]

Most adults used to think of teen violence as an urban problem. "It's those kids in the gangs. They're out doing drive-bys and killing each other." The problem was "out there." It was "their" problem. But what grabbed our attention was that each of these school shooters was a white, middle-class male. They were not from the 'hood or the barrio; they were from suburbs and small towns. The problem is evident throughout our country. It's everyone's problem now, whether we live in an urban center, a farm, or the suburbs. We can no longer pretend it can't happen where we live. I used to worry about our daughters going on mission trips to foreign countries; now I worry about them going to school.

Security in Suburbia

Almost every day a kid gets shot in L.A. What about him? What about the victims in Houston, D.C., Chicago, New York, and Detroit? The media has routinely overlooked African Americans, Latinos, Asian Americans, and other minority teen victims. We do not hear about them, or if we do, they are dismissed in dehumanized terms: "An alleged gang member from the inner city was killed in a vicious attack, an apparent revenge. Film at eleven." We don't inquire about his emotional life or try to understand what happened. We stereotype urban youths and also dismiss them. They do not count. "Just another victim of senseless violence."

When would violence be full of sense? Isn't all violence *senseless?*

When the *senseless violence* hits the suburbs and involves white kids, the public cries out. "How could it happen here?"

James Garbarino, author of *Lost Boys: Why Our Sons Turn Violent and How We Can Save Them,* writes about the recent school shootings: "The killings in the small towns and suburbs during the 1997-1998 school year have served as a kind of wake-up call for America. But this is also an opportunity for Americans to wake up to the fact that the terrible phenomenon of youth violence has been commonplace for the past twenty years and to learn from the experiences of those who have lived with this problem for the last two decades."[10]

What used to be *their* problem is now *our* problem. Let's face it: We are dealing with an epidemic of teen violence.

❖ One-third of adolescent male students nationwide carry a gun, a pocketknife, or some form of weapon to school.

❖ Gunshot wounds are now the second-leading cause of accidental death among ten- to fourteen-year-old males.

❖ Depression in male adolescents is often covert, overlooked when it is displayed through violence, criminal activity, substance abuse, or isolation.

❖ In 1995, 84 percent of all counties in the United States recorded no youth homicides. A sense of immunity that may have prevailed no longer exists.

The teen homicide rate increased nearly 200 percent in the 1990s. The teen suicide rate has increased 400 percent since 1950. According to one Centers for Disease Control and Prevention (CDC) survey of youth, 15 percent of high school boys—whose lethality is much higher than girls—seriously considered suicide in 1997. Boys use guns while girls tend to use pills.[11]

Vulnerable and Violent

Our teenagers are vulnerable and becoming increasingly violent. Why do some teens act out their anger, while others process it and do not react in violence? Consider Dr. James Garbarino's point:

> More children and youth across the country are experiencing the specific negative influences that increase the risk of youth violence. Where and when these negative influences show themselves in actual acts of

aggression may differ from group to group. For example, the kids who committed the infamous school shootings in the 1997-1998 school year killed and injured multiple victims in a single incident and did not have some secondary criminal motive such as robbery or drug dealing. This is different from most of the lethal violence committed by inner-city kids. Also, while for most middle-class teenagers school is a very important social setting and what goes on there is of vital emotional significance, for many inner-city kids, in contrast, school has lost its significance by the time they reach adolescence . . . and they have already dropped out. But once the shooting stops, the net result is the same for parents, friends, teachers, and civic leaders who must cope with the aftermath.

Epidemics tend to start among the most vulnerable segments of the population and then work their way outward, like ripples in a pond. These vulnerable populations don't cause the epidemic. Rather, *their disadvantaged position makes them a good host for the infection.*[12]

The most disadvantaged teens are from the inner cities, but all teens are vulnerable to the same destructive elements. The cries are the same whether they come from the inner city or the suburbs. Teens are crying for protection. They want safety.

It Could Happen Again

I asked some high school guys, "Do you think we'll see another school shooting?"

"Definitely."

"Absolutely."

"It's just a matter of time."

"Do you think it could be a copy-cat challenge, to try to top the number of people shot or killed?"

"Sure. Those guys are so whacked. It's a game to them."

"Like some shoot-em-up video game. 'Watch me nail twenty-eight people!'"

"There are losers like that on every campus."

"Even yours?" I asked.

"Yeah, we know some guys who are tweaked enough to do it."

"But, what about the guys who could but who seem normal to us?" challenged his friend. "They could be in one of our classes, and we would never suspect them."

They paused to scan by memory the faces of their classmates. I noticed the tension rise. The fear was real. *One of our classmates could be a killer!*

A Gallup poll indicates that 79 percent of those surveyed felt that the shooting rampage at Columbine High School in Littleton, Colorado, is an indication of serious problems, compared to only 17 percent who see the event as an isolated incident. At the same time, only a bare majority of the public—53 percent—express confidence that government and society can do anything to prevent similar acts of violence in the future. In fact, two-thirds consider it likely that a similar incident could happen in their own community.[13]

Our teens are indeed facing serious problems.

Millennials and adults differ in their opinions on what causes school violence.

> The findings of a new Gallup Youth Survey show first and foremost that teens think the blame for school violence, in essence, lies within the social structure that dominates today's school scene. When asked directly to explain why they feel the Columbine tragedy occurred, 40 percent of teenagers give a response that, in one way

or the other, focuses on problems of peer relations and peer pressures. The types of responses grouped in this category include the observations that students are taunted by other students, that they are picked on, that they are made to feel like outcasts, that they feel left out, that they have been pushed too far, and that they are lonely. The second category of explanations for Columbine, used by 16 percent of teenagers in the survey, included comments focused on the perpetrators themselves: that they had personal problems, that they were sick, angry, confused, jealous, or "stupid." Another 7 percent of teenagers talked about the fact that warning signals were ignored by those involved, while 4 percent mentioned factors relating to the parents.[14]

Millennials feel that the blame for school violence lies more with themselves and school social structures than with parents, guns, or media violence. Adults look at school violence quite differently. They are more apt to fault parental involvement and responsibility (32 percent), a lack of security at schools (16 percent), better gun control/laws/issues (12 percent), or the need for more counseling support from the schools (6 percent) as causes for school violence.[15]

When 1,073 adults were asked, "In your opinion, why did the shooting at Littleton happen?" The Gallup Organization reported the results:[16]

Causes of School Shootings—According to Adults

Cause	Percentage
parents, family	45
personal problems	11
lack of morals/religion	8
media violence	6

These findings reveal more than statistics. Millennials think relationally and personally, while their parents think psychologically and systemically. Millennials want better school security (24 percent, the largest single category of responses) and so do their parents (16 percent). Regarding the causes of school violence, students tend to look within themselves and at their peers, while adults tend to place blame on other adults and society at large.

When 403 millennials, aged thirteen to seventeen, were asked, "In your opinion, why did the shooting at Littleton happen?" The Gallup Organization reported these results:[17]

Causes of School Shootings—According to Teens

Cause	Percentage
peer issues	40
personal problems	16
warning signs ignored	7
parents, family	4

Teenagers ranked parents and family as the fourth reason for the shootings, while their parents ranked this cause the highest (45 percent). Noticeably absent from the teen list—but included among the top four for parents—were lack of morals/religion and media violence.

When they were asked, "In your opinion, what could be done to reduce the likelihood of a situation like this happening at your own school?" teens responded with these answers:[18]

Teens' Suggestions to Reduce School Violence

Cause	Percentage
better security	24
counseling and communication	18
getting along, tolerance	18
awareness	10

Remarkably, parents did not mention peer issues, but millennials describe it as the number one cause for the rampage. Millennials did not mention a lack of morals or religion, but they did respond with the need to get along and be tolerant. To many, the new religion is tolerance. In a value-free, relativistic culture, the only thing not tolerated is a belief in absolutes: Honesty is always right, do to others what you want them to do to you, and other such values are seen as old-fashioned and moralistic. Yet high moral standards are essential as boundaries in a tumultuous culture. Standards give our teens guidance and can protect their innocence. Moral standards add security to their shaky world. When millennials ask for better security, counseling, and communication as ways to reduce the chance of school violence, they are asking for protection and guidelines. They are asking for borders.

As parents, we need to be adult enough to set and uphold the borders—for our kid's sake. Many boomer parents have been too self-absorbed and too busy to set standards and reinforce them with their teens. They do not want to be seen as uncool or old-fashioned, but in their zeal to be hip, they have left their teens unprotected. Because of their own insecurities, they have created a climate that breeds insecurity. Many of us feel inept to be parents—especially parents of teenagers. We don't have the tools, the examples, or on many days, the energy to deal with the challenge of parenting teens.

I do not leave unpunished the sins of those who hate me, but I punish the children for the sins of their parents to the third and fourth generations. (Exodus 20:5 NLT)

I like what Michael and Diane Medved suggest:

Strong standards not only work to curb societal ills, but also answer a growing call for greater accountability for youth. The New York research organization, Public Agenda, surveyed adults and concluded, "Americans are convinced that today's adolescents face a crisis—not in their economic or physical well-being but in their values and morals." Nine out of ten adults said that the failure to learn values is widespread, and only 19 percent said that parents are commonly good role models. Half of the adults polled said that it is very common for parents to fail to discipline their children. Asked to describe today's teens, two-thirds offered negative terms, such as *rude, wild,* and *irresponsible.* A full half came up with *spoiled* to describe younger children; nearly a third chose the word *lazy.* The Public Agenda study suggests that children are not the only ones who need limits on their behavior. *We* need limits on children, to make our *own* lives freer from problems and more refined. Children's security doesn't come from watered-down values instruction offered in schools (though schools should reinforce and respect the values kids learn from their parents). Kids need the consistency of limits set in their own homes, from their earliest years They need to know what's expected of them on an array of basics: in terms of respect for elders, in terms of their responsibilities in the family, in terms of courtesies and kindness.[19]

Building Security into Our Teens' Lives

As people of faith, we have a distinct advantage when it comes to building security into our teens' lives. The process does not have to depend entirely on us. We can help our daughters and sons discover that true security does not lie in metal detectors, intervention programs at school, or community resources and activities. True security lies in a personal relationship with an almighty, sovereign God. Nothing surprises God. He does not wake up one morning and wring His hands, wondering, "Oh my! What shall I do?"

The best way to create a secure environment that helps teens mature at a natural pace is to reinforce their faith in God. God goes everywhere. Our teens may not want us to tag along with them, but they can understand that God goes everywhere with them. This, by the way, is helpful for accountability as well as safety!

Continue to work with the school and the community to make your neighborhood safe. Continue to build fences and boundaries on the home front that will protect your children. But be certain that you spend some precious time and energy introducing your teen to God and helping him grow in faith. This is the single most effective strategy we have to help our teens feel safe.

Consider the following biblical principles:

* *God is our refuge.* "He who fears the LORD has a secure fortress, and for his children it will be a refuge." (Proverbs 14:26 NIV)

* *God is our protector.* "For he guards the course of the just and protects the way of his faithful ones." (Proverbs 2:8 NIV)

* *God is our powerful Shepherd.* "See, the Sovereign LORD comes with power, and his arm rules for him. See, his reward is with him, and his recompense accompanies him. He tends his flock like a shepherd: He gathers the lambs in

his arms and carries them close to his heart; he gently leads those that have young." (Isaiah 40:10-11 NIV)

When we build these powerful concepts into the lives of our teens, we are building emotional and spiritual fences of protection into their lives. Fences of protection don't lead to bondage; they lead to freedom.

I run in the path of your commands, for you have set my heart free. (Psalm 119:32 NIV)

Establishing Stability

The day after the September 11 atrocity, I was asked to offer a seminar for parents and children to help them talk about terrorism, suffering, and war. We opened the seminar to the community and sixty-eight attended. Most of the people were from our church, but sixteen came from the community. Christina was one of these guests.

"How did you hear about our seminar?" I asked.

"My neighbor told me about it. She knew I was concerned about my kids."

"I'm glad that you came."

"I had to be in a place where people pray. I wanted my children to be around people who pray."

Christina dabbed at a tear forming in her eye. She glanced past me, down the church hallway. "I don't go to church, but for some reason I want to be here. I want my children to be here. I feel safe here. I am a single mom who is barely making it financially, and now I'm barely making it emotionally."

"You and your family are welcome here. I hope you find this to be a safe place."

"It already is, and I've only been here once. Thanks for helping me learn to be stable in a very scary time."

Stability. How do you develop it during insecure times? Here is the core of what I shared with Christina and the others that night.

To help our children feel secure we need S.T.A.B.I.L.I.T.Y.

These factors are especially important following trauma or loss.

SHARE your feelings with your child. Encourage her to share her feelings with you.

TIME—Spend extra time with your child. Slow down and avoid being rushed. Eliminate unnecessary trips, projects, and activities.

ASSURE your child that he is safe and that you will do all you can to keep him safe. Affirm his feelings as normal in an abnormal situation.

BALANCE—Set limits on accessing media that focus on violence and terrorism or other fear-producing sources.

INFORM your child with accurate facts, presented honestly and appropriately for her age.

LISTEN to your child. Tune into verbal and nonverbal cues.

INITIATE family safety procedures to help your children feel prepared the next time an emergency occurs. Preparation and discussion help children feel empowered.

TOUCH—Increase the amount of appropriate touch you offer your child. Even a hug communicates love and security to children.

YOU determine normalcy. Seek to return your family to as normal a routine as possible. You set the tone by the behavior you model.

Security for many teens means having parents "be there" emotionally and physically. We discovered in chapter 2, The Cry for Love, that one love key is touch. I think it is a tragedy when—just as teens need affirming touch the most—parents stop expressing physical affection. There is substantial power in physical closeness and presence. We need to discover appropriate ways to express physical affection to our teenagers. Sometimes a hug, holding hands, or a quick kiss on the forehead can make a significant statement: *I love you, and everything is going to be alright.*

Broken Fences

My wife, Suzanne, and I went to a PG-13 movie that was probably close to deserving an R rating. I didn't know too much about the movie except that it was recommended by some of our friends as a fun date movie because it was a romantic comedy with some proven actors. We plopped down into the reclining seats with cup holders and got ready for fun. The lights dimmed, and the trailers for the upcoming attractions began. A man and woman noisily paraded in with their eight-year-old son in tow. Of course, they sat in front of us. The movie was funny, but it was inappropriate for a third grader. I was uncomfortable seeing these parents expose their son to the sexual themes and adult situations in the movie. *Don't they know better?*

In our desire to be more modern or tolerant or politically correct, we have unwittingly contributed to the lostness of our own children. Thinking that we need to prepare them instead of protect them has led us to expose children to adult problems and activities prematurely. Since we are not comfortable with adolescence, we rush our children through it. Instead of defining it as the last and a protected stage of childhood, we look at teens as mini-adults. We rush them out of childhood and into the cold, real world where they are unprepared to deal with the stress. As a result, millennials feel rejected, even abandoned by their parents, which makes them angry. Some become hostile.

According to a recent Gallup poll:

> As many as four in ten teenagers think that at some
> point in their lifetimes, someone is likely to fire a gun
> at them. Four in ten teens are fearful of walking alone

at night in certain areas within a mile of their homes. Half say they will at some point be mugged. Many factors may contribute to a loss of security and a climate of violence. Teens report possible causes:

+ *Peer pressure.* More than one-third of teens say they are under a "great deal" or "some" pressure from their peers to break rules. Many report being teased about their appearance and clothes.

+ *Attitudes of adults.* Half of teens say they receive "too little" respect from adults, and many feel that they are misunderstood.

+ *Physical abuse.* One teen in eight reports that he has been physically abused—that is, intentionally harmed by beating, hitting, kicking, and so on, out of anger rather than play.

+ *Community to blame.* Many teens fault their communities for not doing more to provide counseling and mentoring for young people.

+ *Missing parents.* One-third of teens cannot talk about "life with father." When asked what relatives live at home with them, although 91 percent say their mother, only 67 percent say their father.

+ *Alienated.* One in five teens fall into the category of "alienated," as determined by the Gallup Youth Survey scale. As many as one teen in ten is willing to admit that they are not happy with the way they are.

+ *Spiritual vacuum.* Only 13 percent of teens say people their age are influenced a "great deal" by religion. Twice as many teens turn to themselves to answer the problems of life as teens who turn to God.

✤ *Too much TV.* Seven in ten teens admit that they spend too much time in front of the tube.

✤ *Dangerous music.* Six in ten teenagers believe gangsta rap encourages violence.

✤ *Living dangerously.* Four in ten teens say they "like to live dangerously"; 48 percent say they like to "shock people"; one-third (36 percent) "worry a lot about death."[20]

Assault on Innocence

The culture in the main no longer supports the family as a viable unit. In fact, our society does not protect the family, nor does it affirm child rearing as a noble task. Our culture does more to undermine our traditional roles as parents and the natural connectedness between family members. I agree with Michael and Diane Medved, who assert there is a national assault on the innocence of our children. All of our children feel it. Some of our children fight back. Some do it with automatic weapons.

My heart was saddened as I watched an *NBC Today* interview with Nicole Nowlen, one of the survivors of the shootings at Columbine High School. The interviewer asked, "Do you remember much from the horrible day, April 20, 1999?"

"Yes, I remember a lot. I could talk with you for two hours about it. People are surprised how much I remember, but I remember it all. I mean, how could I forget? I was in the library when Eric and Dylan came in shooting. I was in the wrong place at the wrong time. They came up to the table where we were sitting and they shot us . . ." Her voice trailed off as she brought the scene to her memory. Her lip quivered, "I was shot nine times in the stomach."

"How are you doing now? I mean, you look like you've completely recovered," said the interviewer.

"I'm doing very well. I don't have problems like some people, like not being able to sleep and other problems."

"You're doing well physically. How are you emotionally?"

"I'm doing very well. Of course, I won't really know until I go to school tomorrow. That's the first day of school. It might be scary being back at Columbine."

"What will be different?"

"I'm different now. I'm no longer innocent and naïve. I liked it better when I was."

Discussion Questions

PARENT TO PARENT

1. What does *security* mean to you?

2. *Time* magazine admitted the news media are afraid because they think they should have answers. What do you think about their admission?

3. What should we do about the epidemic of youth violence? What can you do in your community?

4. Are our teens facing a moral crisis? Explain your thoughts.

5. How can we protect our children's and teens' innocence?

TALKING WITH YOUR TEEN

1. Do teens need stability? What do stability and security look like?

2. Why do you think some students bring weapons to school?

3. Do you think a school shooting could happen at your school? Do you have an idea of who might be capable of carrying out a school shooting? Share your thoughts.

4. How are we as a family, doing with the nine S.T.A.B.I.L.I.T.Y. factors? What suggestions do you have for doing better?

5. Read Proverbs 14:26. Discuss how family faith can be a refuge in unstable times.

Responding to the Cry

THE CRY

The cry for security.

THE CHALLENGE

To create a secure environment in which our teens can mature at a healthy and natural pace.

TOOLS TO USE AT HOME

1. Discuss with your teen what she should do in various unsafe scenarios. For ideas, refer to the chart on the next page.

2. Make a security collage by gluing magazines and newspaper clippings on cardboard. Both parent and teen can make one without looking at each other's until finished. Then discuss the similarities and contrasts between them.

3. Do a safety audit of your home.

   ✤ Are all firearms locked in a cabinet or is access restricted with trigger locks?

   ✤ If you have alcohol in the home, do you restrict access or monitor it to see if minors are using it?

   ✤ Are you careful to keep habit-forming prescription pills away from children?

Preparing for Unsafe Scenarios

Scenario	Plan	Place	Contact
1. You are physically threatened at school	*Report to Principal*	*Office*	*Call parent*
2. You are intimidated or challenged to fight outside of school			
3. You are sexually harassed at school			
4. You are sexually harassed away from school			
5. Someone brings a weapon to school			
6. A terrorist attack occurs in the community			
7. You find evidence of a hate crime			
8. You find tagging or vandalism			
9. A shooting occurs at school			
10. Other _____			

✤ Do you keep solvents, glue, spray paint, and other inhalants under lock and key?

✤ Have you checked your smoke alarm, door locks, and window latches to make sure they are operational?

✤ Do you have names and numbers of neighbors posted so that your children can call for help, if they need to?

4. Do a technology check of your home.

✤ How do you monitor technology use in your home?

✤ Do you have screening software on your computer to keep kids out of adult sites, inappropriate chat rooms, and Web sites that may promote hate or violence?

❖ Have you checked the history on your Internet browser to see if anyone is misusing it?

❖ How do you restrict access to TV, especially if you have cable or satellite access?

❖ Discuss standards for computer, TV, and phone use with your family. Consider posting the rules along with an appropriate verse such as Psalm 51:10 or Psalm 101:3.

5. Make your home emotionally safe. Discuss what it means to honor and respect each other. Read Ephesians 4:29-32 and 6:1-4. Brainstorm behaviors that are dishonoring and disrespectful. Decide on a consequence for family members who are disrespectful of others. One family assigns the humble chore of picking up the dog messes for a week if anyone shows dishonor or disrespect. Even the parents might have to do it.

TOOLS TO USE AT CHURCH

1. In your parents-of-teens group, compare family standards for media, curfew, dating, and parties. Explain reasoning behind the standards and how the standards are reinforced. In other words, "How do you check up on your teens to make sure they follow the rules?"

2. Discuss with another parent where you are on the *prepare-versus-protect* continuum.

3. Using a concordance and a thesaurus, look up words in the Bible that have to do with security: *stable, faithful, reliable, trustworthy, dependable,* and others. What visual images of security do you find? For example, "The LORD is my rock . . .

in whom I take refuge" (Psalm 18:2). How might you pass these biblical images to your teen? Perhaps you can find a river rock (or purchase one from the home improvement store) and write Psalm 18:2 on it. Give it to your teen.

4. Develop a mentoring program at your church so that each teen who wants one can have a caring and trained adult with whom he or she feels secure. For resources, check out *www.uyt.com.*

5. Gather parents of your teen's friends. Develop as many common standards and expectations as possible so the teens don't play parent against parent. "Well, Vanessa's parents let her stay out until one in the morning. Don't you trust me? Why do I have to be in at eleven?" The parent response: "I've talked to Vanessa's mom, and we both agree on eleven for most weeknights and twelve for special times like the prom."

CHAPTER 4

A Cry for Purpose

You ou mean to tell me that I can combine surfing with telling people about God? Cool!"

"Yeah," I responded to Luis as we sat on our surfboards, waiting for the next set of waves. "You can combine your passion for surfing with your passion for missions. You don't have to give up one for the other."

"How?"

"There's a group that takes surfers to other countries to surf, hang out with the locals, and tell them about Christ."

"Are they legit? They aren't some random deal? My folks are going to want to know."

"Absolutely, dude. You can check out their Web site. Remember Alejandro and Justin went to Australia last summer? It was with this group."

"I'm stoked! Now I know what I'm going to do next summer after I graduate." He smiled, plopped down on his board, and paddled toward the peak on the horizon.

Our teenagers long to be part of a grand story. Their hearts crave to be characters in a story that matters—one with creative design, passionate characters, and a noble mission. The craving is diminished by tragedies, materialism, and the frantic pace of our culture, but it isn't destroyed. Some call this hunger "the longing for transcendence," the passion to be something larger than ourselves and out of the ordinary. If you are willing to make the effort, you will discover that beneath the adolescent façade is a heart crying for a sense of purpose. The fourth cry of today's teens is to have some form of heroic purpose.

The cry for purpose is the need for adventure, meaning, and intimacy.

America's teenagers see themselves contributing to a better world in the new century upon us—a world with less racial discrimination, a world more concerned about the needs of the less fortunate, a world that is less polluted and more caring about the environment, a more peaceful world with fewer wars and armed conflicts. And finally, teenagers see themselves contributing to a world of new hope and sense of purpose.

—George Gallup Jr.

Adolescent Adventure

Today's teens are searching for a cause to embrace. They are looking for an adventure that demands something from them. So much of their lives have been sanitized from risk and harm that they are looking for ways to "be on the edge" or "push the envelope." This helps explain why millennials have such a high interest in missions. They are willing to give up comfort for a quest with purpose. Some millennials are simply looking for an experience such as snowboarding in the Andes. But when the experience can be supported with an admirable purpose —say, snowboarding in the Andes to build relationships with South

American teens in order to present Christ to them—then it becomes an adventure.

Without a sense of purpose, teens are left to pursue adventure in less noble ways. Consider Charles Colson's observation: "The naturalistic view of life pervades every area of Western culture, but nowhere with greater effect than among young people. At every turn, they are bombarded with hedonistic, self-gratifying messages. Day in and day out, they are bombarded with the message that life is all about toys and pleasures and satisfying every hormonal urge."[1]

It only takes a few minutes of MTV to see what Colson is talking about. Consistent messages of hedonism reinforce the naturalistic philosophy of a beer commercial in the minds of our teens every hour of every day: *You only live once, so grab all the pleasure you can.*

If we don't offer our young people noble adventures, they tend to settle for hedonistic diversions.

Millennial Meaning

Millennials are in pursuit of meaning. They are looking for clarity in their lives. Having been raised in the relativistic fog of our "anything goes" culture, they are searching for a guiding light they can depend on. Many of today's teens lack a clear sense of meaning for their lives. They are searching for a meaningful cause they can support. They are longing for purpose and an understanding of where they came from and why they are here. It's easy to see why our teens express a cry for purpose. Life has no purpose when people have no understanding of their origin or destination.

The late philosopher and author Dr. Francis Schaeffer described it accurately: "The dilemma of modern man is simple: He does not know why man has any meaning . . . this is the damnation of our generation, the heart of modern man's problem."[2]

I was surprised that 91.6 percent of the teens surveyed in our Gallup Cries of Teens Poll indicated that it was an "important" need or "very important" need to *believe that life is meaningful and has purpose.* I had just assumed that everybody had worked through the issues of purpose and that we needed to move on to other, weightier topics, but I was wrong. This is why we do surveys: to correct our biases and become more accurate in our understandings of what people feel and need.

Our teens do indeed struggle with the absence of meaning in life. They are confused. Having grown up in schools that have taught naturalism and humanism, they are not equipped to deal with what is sometimes called "first truths." The relativistic popular culture criticizes any form of absolutes, so any attempt at defining and promoting universal truths is resisted, if not ridiculed. Teens are vainly searching to satisfy the hunger of their souls for purpose.

> Everything still to come is meaningless. Young man, it's wonderful to be young! Enjoy every minute of it. Do everything you want to do; take it all in. But remember that you must give an account to God for everything you do. So banish grief and pain, but remember that youth, with a whole life before it, still faces the threat of meaninglessness. Don't let the excitement of youth cause you to forget your Creator. Honor him in your youth before you grow old and no longer enjoy living. (Ecclesiastes 11:8–12:1 NLT)

The search for meaning continues from the day of Ecclesiastes. We have a unique opportunity to speak to this need. The culture has shifted. For the first time in years, many Americans are willing to admit that personal morality has public consequences. From the Monica Lewinsky–Bill Clinton scandal to the schoolyard massacres to the terrorist attacks of 2001 and the executive indulgences and moral lapses that tanked corporations, we have ample evidence that personal morality has a huge impact on the public. The comfortable modern notion of individual autonomy has proven to be heinously vacant. The choices that we make as individuals *do* matter. Our thinking and our choices *do* have consequences. Individuals making choices based on what *they* think is right has led to a loss of community and civility. It has left us desperately searching for answers, not more questions. When we embrace choice over morality, we produce chaos.

As a result, Americans are groping for something that will restore the shattered bonds of family and community, something that will make sense of life. If the church turns inward now, if we focus only on our own needs, we will miss the opportunity to provide answers at a time when people are sensing a deep longing for meaning and order.[3]

Our teens are expressing this deep longing for meaning. They are crying for specific answers to cosmic questions:

- Where did we come from? (question of origin)

- How did God design us? (question of design)

- What has gone wrong? (question of morality)

- How can we fix what is wrong? (question of theology)

- What should we be doing? (question of duty)

- What lies beyond? (question of destiny)

In contrast to secular humanism, new age beliefs, and other modern views, only Christianity provides valid and credible answers to the cosmic questions. Charles Colson aptly writes: "Only Christianity offers a way to understand both the physical and the moral order. Only Christianity offers a comprehensive worldview that covers all areas of life and thought, every aspect of creation. Only Christianity offers a way to live in the real world."[4]

September 11, 2001, was a wake-up call for many drowsy Americans. Previously our lives were focused on happiness, achievement, acquisition, or power. For many, their lives had no aim or purpose. Many moderns have lost any sense of a higher destiny. Each pursuit proves empty because it fails to answer the cosmic question—the query of purpose:

> What is the purpose of life?
> *To live according to the design of our Creator.*

The key to teenagers' restless hearts is to help them discover how to live by fulfilling God's purpose in their lives. By approaching life with this worldview, we deal with the macro questions, "Where did I come from? Where am I going?"

Our teens are fervently in search of purpose for their lives. They want an adventure with a cause. They want a mission with meaning. They want to be close to others with the same passion.

Intentional Intimacy

The cry for purpose is the need for adventure, meaning, and intimacy. For today's teens, intimacy needs to be purposeful and sincere. Millennials are looking for intimacy that is intentional, not casual or accidental.

Intimacy is knowing the inmost character or essence of a person, being familiar with someone's heart, two souls being at home with each other. Intimacy says, "There is room in my heart for you." When we hear the word *intimacy,* we may be tempted to think of the allure of sex, but true intimacy is much more than sex. It is an unembarrassed authenticity that says, "What we are together is too important for me to pretend I am something I am not." Authenticity does not have value in itself. Its value only becomes real in relationship.

Millennials are crying out to be included. They don't want to be left out. With too-busy parents and too few mentors, they have been marginalized. They need us to make room in our lives for them.

Jesus promises purpose by promising intimacy.

> Don't be troubled. You trust God, now trust in me.
> There are many rooms in my Father's home, and I am
> going to prepare a place for you. If this were not so, I
> would tell you plainly. When everything is ready, I
> will come and get you, so that you will always be with
> me where I am. (John 14:1-3 NLT)

Jesus is not simply saving a place for us at the table; he is building the table, the dining room, and the house that one day will be ours.

Thanksgiving at our house often includes a card table for the children since there is not enough room for everyone at the fancy table in the dining room. It was fun for our daughters when they were younger, but when they became teenagers they didn't like to be relegated to the kids' table.

When we enjoy the wedding feast of the Lamb in heaven, we each will have a chair at the table. There will be a place setting and a name card for each name! We won't have to sit at the kids' table in the kitchen. We will be sitting with our Bridegroom—the One who has been preparing a place for us. Why?

Because He wants us to be with Him.

Nobody wants to be left out. I remember the agony of third grade recess. Each of us stood in line like chuck roasts in the butcher store, while the captains of the opposing softball teams chose the prime cuts and the choice meats, descending from the most desirable to the least. I was never the first to be chosen and often was the last.

"I don't want Smith; I had him last time."

"Okay, four-eyes, come with me. I'm stuck with you. Try not to drop the ball."

I felt like discount hamburger.

But that is not the way it is with Jesus. He says, "I'm making a place for you. You'll be with me, and it's going to be out of this world!"

Perhaps a glimpse of heaven is when we enter a room and someone exclaims, "Hey, over here! I've saved a place for you. I'm glad you're here." Joy is having someone save a place for you.

Within the heart of every teenager is a yearning for purpose—for adventure, meaning, and intimacy.

I think C. S. Lewis captured it best: "If I find in myself desires which nothing in this world can satisfy, the only logical explanation is that I was made for another world."[5]

A Biblical View of Purpose

Felicia left her biology class confused about what Mrs. Radcliffe had just taught about origins. "We are examples of millions and millions of cells self-organizing and evolving over millions and millions of years," claimed the teacher as she pointed to the chart above the white board that illustrated evolution from a one-celled organism to fish to frogs and eventually to humans.

It didn't seem right to Felicia. Everything she had learned at her church seemed to contradict what she was being taught in biology. *Where will I get some answers? If God loves us and has a plan, why did He have to use evolution to eventually get around to it?*

If Felicia were your daughter, what would you tell her?

Would you think to tell her that evidence for design is found throughout the physical universe and that if the universe appears to be designed, it *is* designed? Are you prepared to counter some of the naturalistic, humanistic explanations that your teenager is likely to encounter at school? Consider the graph on the next page and use it to strengthen your teen's sense of purpose.

In our culture so much emphasis has been on *self-esteem,* but our teens need more than good feelings about themselves. They need to understand that God designed them to be unique and wonderfully complex. We can help our teens develop a sense of destiny that

Discovering Purpose

Design

✛ God made us according to His master plan.

✛ "You made all the delicate, inner parts of my body and knit me together in my mother's womb. Thank you for making me so wonderfully complex! Your workmanship is marvelous—and how well I know it." (Psalm 139:13-14 NLT)

✛ We were created by intelligent design rather than natural process (evolution). We aren't mistakes; we are masterpieces. We are creations of worth.

Destiny

✛ We discover our purpose and future in relationship with God.

✛ "For I know the plans I have for you," says the LORD. "They are plans for good and not for disaster, to give you a future and a hope." (Jeremiah 29:11 NLT)

✛ Each of us has a soul with a unique shape that fits God. Each of us has a unique, creative contribution to make. We are God's people.

Duty

✛ We can offer service to God and others.

✛ "God has given gifts to each of you from his great variety of spiritual gifts. Manage them well so that God's generosity can flow through you." (1 Peter 4:10 NLT)

✛ We are valuable to the mission and purpose God has planned. Our service has eternal consequences.

points to a future with hope. We can also help them see that they are valuable and that they have something of value to contribute when they serve.

If we can do this, we are providing what our teens need: a noble adventure, a mission with meaning, and others to join them in the quest.

THE ENCOURAGING WORD
Biblically Boosting Your Teen

Let your teen know God loves him. Help shape his sense of purpose with a biblical worldview. The Bible is full of encouraging passages. Try writing some of them on slips of paper and placing them on your teen's pillow once a week. Or tape them on a mirror your teen uses. Here are a few encouraging verses to get you started.[6]

PSALM 52:8	God's love is unfailing.
PSALM 91:14-16	God is with us in trouble.
PSALM 117:2	Great is God's love toward us.
ISAIAH 43:1-3	Do not fear.
JEREMIAH 31:3	God's love is everlasting.
JEREMIAH 33:3	God will answer our prayers.
LAMENTATIONS 3:22-23	God is faithful.
HABAKKUK 1:5	God is doing something amazing.
ROMANS 8:38-39	We cannot be separated from God's love.
EPHESIANS 3:17-18	Christ's love is huge.
1 JOHN 3:1	We are God's kids.

A Longing for a Spiritual Experience

Interwoven throughout each of the Seven Cries is a longing for a spiritual experience, but it stands out dramatically as we consider the millennials' quest for meaning. Our findings indicate four aspects of this cry:

1: THE SPIRITUAL SPLITS

Most millennials believe the Bible is accurate but reject many of the key teachings. They see the Bible as a menu of stories, ones that they can pick and choose to apply to their life as they see fit—a spiritual *soup de jour*. Most teens are familiar with biblical principles but do not apply them consistently. Here again is evidence of their patchwork thinking, which is an eclectic mixture of contradictory beliefs. Perhaps their incongruent thinking is a result of a hectic, discordant lifestyle. Many millennials are too busy to reflect. They simply do not have the time to notice the inconsistencies. As a result, they end up with a blend of beliefs—what some have called "mosaic morality."

2: ENVIRONMENTAL SPIRITUALITY

Their environment dramatically affects millennials' spirituality. If they are around others who are committed to Bible study, sharing, and prayer, they will be reflecting a life of Bible study, sharing, and prayer. If they socialize primarily with teens who simply attend church, then that will be the extent of their spiritual experience. Millennials are *spiritual chameleons*; they adapt to the environment they find them-selves in. One constant in the life of every millennial is change. They have quickly learned to adapt to change. That is why it appears that they have hot and cold enthusiasm for spiritual disciplines. Just as the windshield wipers on your car have an intermittent setting, millenni-als have a setting for intermittent spiritual discipline.

3: UNREALIZED SPIRITUAL POTENTIAL

Millennials are on a quest for spiritual experience. They are more open to this than their parents realize. In fact, they are looking to their parents for dialogue, for content, and for direction on spiritual issues. But most parents are strangely silent on this topic. They ratio-nalize, *I take the kid to youth group. Isn't that enough?* Our research indicates that parents have the greatest influence on their teen's spir-itual vitality, in spite of parents investing little time to discuss it. Why? Because most teens emulate what they see their parents doing. What would happen if parents were intentional and had a plan to build their teen's spiritual depth and maturity? Even teens who do not have Christian parents are open to a spiritual mentor—a youth worker or Sunday school teacher who takes a personal interest in them and their spiritual journeys.

4: THE EMERGENCE OF SPIRITUAL HEROES

William Strauss, coauthor of *The Fourth Turning,* predicts that millennials will be a generation of heroes. In a 1996 interview, he said, "You watch, at the turn of the millennium magazine covers will be proclaiming that they are a wonderful generation—not so much for who they are but for who the nation wants them to be."[7]

And that is exactly what happened: *Time, Newsweek, USA Today,* and other national periodicals all displayed cover stories in the last few years on "how good these teens are." Millennials are a paradoxical generation. Some teens are out shooting up their world while others are trying to save it.

Wendy Murray Zoba aptly describes this spiritual heroism:

> The constancy, speed, and shock levels of so much of the world millennials inhabit have honed them to operate in extremes, boldly and unabashedly. Moral ambiguity has spurred them to want decisive boundaries and real answers. Spiritual longing has made them ready to give it everything they've got in their quest for God. In other words, they will do things *in the extreme.* When they answer the call to heroism, they will answer it boldly. When it comes to embracing moral truth, they will do so unabashedly. When they give their lives to the Lord, they will serve with everything on the line. . . . The time is right for parents and the church to seize this season of spiritual ripeness in young people to capture their longings, win their allegiance, and equip them to give every-

thing they've got to carry the "extreme gospel" into the next millennium.[8]

The Lost Boys

A sense of purpose is vital to teenagers, particularly boys. Without a clear sense of purpose teenage boys are more likely to harm themselves or others. It is critical that we provide our boys (and girls) with substance and clarity about the purpose in living. Our responsibility as parents is to nurture their spiritual development. Our boys need to be strong in their faith if they are to understand the meaning of good and evil. Dr. James Dobson writes about purpose and morality:

> [Teens] are growing up in a postmodern world in which all ideas are considered equally valid and nothing is really wrong. Wickedness is bad only in the minds of those who think it is bad. People who live by this godless outlook on life are headed for great pain and misery. The Christian worldview, by contrast, teaches that good and evil are determined by the God of the universe and that He has given us an unchanging moral standard by which to live. He also offers forgiveness from sins, which boys (and girls) have good reason to need. Only with this understanding is a child being prepared to face the challenges that lie ahead. Yet most American children receive no spiritual training whatsoever! They are left to make it up as they go along, which leads to the meaningless existence we have discussed.[9]

Two seemingly ordinary boys from normal middle-class families ambled onto their high school campus at lunch in an affluent suburb of Denver and shot and killed a dozen of their classmates and a teacher before turning their automatic weapons on themselves. The Columbine tragedy captured the attention of the country. It was a watershed moment in our contemporary life, a definitive plummet from innocence. It shocked us all. *It could happen here!* The fear ran rampant through the cul-de-sacs of suburbia.

The barrage of bullets paralleled an outbreak in multiple levels of evil, each one seeming more sinister. It was a fall from innocence and an escalation in hate. The serenity of suburbia was shattered. Parents and teachers began to look at their kids with unfamiliar feelings of anxiety, doubt, and in some cases, suspicion.

What's wrong with these kids? The question was on everybody's minds.

Sure, there had been other school shootings, but Columbine (the name itself quickly became an icon for teen tragedy) penetrated into the soul of America and wreaked havoc with our purpose. The times are good, but something is awfully wrong with America's teens.

What troubles us about Columbine is how ordinary the lives of the shooters were and how extraordinary were their premeditated and vicious acts. It does not add up. We understand violence in inner-city schools. We almost expect it. But Columbine was different. It was a brutal 3:00 A.M. wake-up call. It made us speculate whether we had been in denial about the sickness of the souls of our middle-class teens and their parents.

"What went wrong with these boys?"

"Where were their parents?"

"Did the school or community fail them?"

"Could it happen here?" This perhaps is the most haunting question. The answer, sadly, is yes.

America's teens are suffering alienation, emptiness, and an epidemic lack of purpose. The cry of our teens is for purpose. For some teens their purpose is a mission for meaningfulness; for others it is simply an escape from pain.

Teens are in a stage of development when they take huge risks. Sometimes they take them because they don't know better. Sometimes they take them for thrills. And sometimes they take them to escape pain.

As we more closely observe these angst-ridden adolescents, we can't help but notice the adults in the background. They may not be abusive or neglectful in the conventional sense, but apart from comfortable homes and material goods, they have nothing of substance to pass on to their teens. The school shootings have pulled back the miniblinds of suburbia and let us peek into family lives to discover a spiritual and emotional void. Troubled teens could easily pour their most vicious and hate-filled fantasies into this vacuum. It was a way to escape.

Absent Fathers

Before assuming his current role as a presidential cabinet member, General Colin Powell fought courageously in the Gulf War. Following that campaign, he began another campaign—to combat fatherlessness. He founded America's Promise: The Alliance for Youth, a mentoring program. He says:

> Nearly forty percent of our children are growing up without a father at home. Some sociologists predict this figure could reach fifty percent in the next few years. It is a cruel and often life-warping deprivation.
>
> Teen-age boys without fathers are notoriously prone to crime. Seventy-two percent of adolescent murderers and seventy percent of long-term prison inmates come from fatherless homes. Even if they stay out of jail, fatherless boys still are two to three times more likely to drop out of school or to get divorced in later life.

That boys need fathers is widely recognized. Less so is the fact that girls need them, too. It is unconditional love from their fathers that teaches young women they are worthy of affection and respect from other men. Just as teen-age boys without fathers are two to three times more likely to commit crimes, teenage girls without fathers are two to three times more likely to conceive a child out of wedlock.[10]

The key to building healthy families and teenagers is to have active fathers in the home. Fathers bring purpose, stability, and resources—characteristics often absent in homes without dads.

Some fathers are physically present but not actively involved or emotionally connected with their children. They are emotionally absent. The results are similar to a fatherless home. Teens need fathers who are there *for* them and *with* them—emotionally present fathers.

Some teens return each day to beautiful homes, but no parents. They may have all the marks of success—clothes, video games, cars, cell phones, and computers—but they don't have available and tuned-in parents who can give them feedback and coaching. These part-time parents may be home, but they often are disconnected from their teens. They may eat meals with their teens, but the television probably stays on. These parent figures have extricated themselves from the common task of parenting: guiding and shaping their teens.

I believe that most have done this not because they are too busy at work or distracted by amusement, but because they do not have the tools to do their job. Our culture has not provided the support for parents to pass on any firm values. Instead, our culture offers pluralism, "What is right for you may not be right for me." It is an ethos of nonjudgmental tolerance. The result is a bland, blurred belief system drained of all conviction and power. The rationale has been, "We don't want to force absolutes down our kids throats. We will be more cool and tolerant than that."

So instead of giving teens something, we have given them nothing. In the attempt to be politically correct, we have become morally bankrupt.

I believe that not having values worth fighting for has left many parents without the distinction of being an authority. If everyone's opinion is equally valid, then declaring something a moral absolute is impossible. We can never say to our teens, "I am sorry, but that is wrong." It would be simply opinion. When parents are left to rear their children by opinions only, it erodes their authority over their children. They have become buddies and housemates, and when that happens, childhood must disappear. Childhood cannot exist without any adults around. If everybody is equal, then who is in charge?

There are higher values to pass on to our teens. A higher purpose than achievement or acquisition does exist. As parents who care about their teens, we need to be passionate and intentional about rearing our teens with purpose, character, and values.

Parents abdicate their responsibilities when they cease to nurture the vulnerable young and prepare them for independent life. Parents in particular and adults in general have contributed to the lack of purpose among millennials. The adults in some teens' lives have no substantial emotional and ethical nourishment for filling the empty imaginations of teenagers, nothing to give order to their muddled, embryonic selves. Many of these privileged middle-class kids strike out on their search for meaning, looking to adults for cues, only to discover the adults staring vacantly at the ground.

It's enough to make some of them very angry.

A Road Not Traveled

One of the ways we can help teens is to be available to them as parents and mentors. As adults we can offer the experience of surviving adolescence. We do not have to be experts on psychology, physiology, education, or theology; we simply need to have traveled the road ahead of them. Most teens are open to having a mentor. Eighty-five percent reported in a recent Gallup Youth Survey that it was "very important" for them to "spend regular time with an adult who cares about them, such as a mentor, tutor, or coach."[11] Eighty-five percent! That is almost nine out of ten teens who would like to have some kind of caring connection with an adult. This is one of the remarkable distinctives of the millennial generation. They are open to mentoring.

Sometimes the teen's emotions bubble forth like a cauldron. They are often surprised by their own percolating feelings. Teens cannot always make sense of their emotions. That is why they need guides. If they have someone to help them sort through their feelings, they don't feel abandoned. But if they are left by themselves to venture into unknown territory, ill-equipped and lost, they are likely to become angry—mad about being left alone without the skills to navigate their adolescence. The cry for purpose is a summons for guidance, a desperate call for deliverance from pain, and a plea to discover that life does not have to be cruel, but in fact, it has purpose. Our millennials cry, *Please help me discover that life isn't a cruel joke.*

Our recent survey indicated that "the need to escape pain" was "very strong" among 53 percent of the thirteen- to fifteen-year-old females, with an additional 21 percent reporting that it was a "strong" need in their lives. Seventy-four percent of these girls are very much involved with efforts to avoid pain. This is in stark contrast to boys the same age who report in with 36 percent answering "very strong" and 25 percent responding that escaping pain is a "strong" need in their lives. Why is there such a difference?

It could be that thirteen- to fifteen-year-old young women feel more victimized or at-risk than their male peers. Their male peers are likely contributing to these feelings. It could also be that boys at this age are very much into macho posturing that minimizes weaknesses and almost embraces pain as a rite of passage. Girls tend to be more skilled in understanding their emotions at this stage. Boys tend to run away from their emotions. Some women readers might be thinking, *The same is true of men!*

Our survey confirms that teens need to believe that life is meaningful and has a purpose. For older teenage girls (sixteen to seventeen), this was extremely important, with 89 percent reporting that this was a "very strong" need in their lives, in contrast to 74 percent of the sixteen- to seventeen-year-old boys and 69 percent of the thirteen- to fifteen-year-old boys. Teens who had attended religious services in the past week reported higher than those who did not by ten points. Eight-one percent of the teens who went to religious services say it is a "very strong" need for them to believe that life is meaningful and has a purpose. In contrast, 71 percent of teens who didn't attend religious services report that it is a "very strong" need. *Attending church seems to sharpen teenagers' belief in a meaningful and purposeful life.*[12]

When it comes to the cry for purpose, parents and teens have something in common. Parents do not always know how to give direction and guidance to their teens. Teens do not know how to ask for guidance—or are not even aware they lack it. What both groups need are guides to help teens connect with their parents or mentors.

I began to see a pattern in families with millennials: parents not having the skills to connect with their teens, and teens desperately needing to connect with their parents. Both parents and teens were experiencing angst, but they seldom talked about it—at least not to each other. I researched the issue further and discovered key essential skills and attributes teens need to be capable of to experience purpose in their lives. Attributes include humility, compassion, courage, persistence, responsibility, and passion for God. Life skills include setting moral standards, establishing disciplined study habits, dealing well with emotions, choosing friends, handling finances, maintaining the car, cooking, and organizing personal papers and time.

The following is what I tell teenagers about developing purpose in their lives: "Don't attempt being a teenager alone! You wouldn't try driving without proper instruction—well, you shouldn't! Just like when you learn to drive a car, you need some guidance to help you learn to drive through life, especially the next few years while you're on the teenage turnpike. The idea behind mentoring is to help you connect with your parent or another caring adult. Teens need mentors—someone to coach, encourage, and support them. You may not know it, but you're growing up in a culture that's increasingly dangerous for you." Some examples:

- *Teens are hurried.* Our culture is not comfortable with the teenage years, so we rush our children toward adulthood. Teens are copying the frantic pace of their parents. Today's teens are being robbed of their innocence, exposed to information intended only for adults. They are unprepared and overexposed to the harsh realities in life. They need the protection and guidance of caring adult mentors such as parents and youth workers.

- *Teens are hushed.* Teens lack a voice. Adults are busy with jobs, activities, commitments, mortgages, cell phones, and e-mails. We are drowning in information. With the flood of data, we easily silence or ignore our teenagers. We lack advocates for youth. We need adults to speak up for and speak into the lives of our youth. Mentors are caring adults who value kids enough to spend time with them and listen to them.

- *Teens are hostile.* Across the country we have seen evidence of hostile teens. The school and the church shootings are the most dramatic examples. When teens are *hurried, hassled,* and *hushed,* they become *hostile.*

We who care about teens can choose to connect with them. We can protect them from being hurried. We can value them and show them they have a valid place. We can listen to them and be advocates for their concerns. Or we can ignore them and deal with the hostility that results.[13]

Understanding Versus Agreement

I was talking with an angry teenager last week.

"I understand what you are going through," I said.

"At least somebody does!" He exhaled with frustration.

"I can see that you're really angry."

"Got that right."

"Yeah, I understand what you are facing."

"So you agree with me about my parents and what I want to do?"

"No. I understand, but I don't agree."

He looked at me puzzled. "I thought you understood."

"I do. At least I think I do."

"So why don't you agree?"

"Because understanding doesn't equal agreement."

He kept staring at me like I was speaking Mandarin. "I don't get it."

"Just because I take the time to understand you doesn't mean I'm going to come to the same conclusions you do. Your parents may not understand you, but even if they do, it doesn't mean that they'll agree with you. Understanding and agreement aren't the same."

"Why not?"

"It's unrealistic. Don't aim for agreement. That's impossible. Aim for understanding, and you won't be so disappointed and angry. Hey, sometimes I don't even agree with myself. How can I expect others to always agree with me?"

He smiled, "Yeah. I always thought they were the same, but now I see your point."

In parent-teen relationships, it isn't always possible to have agreement, but we can work toward understanding.

Teens without Purpose

Many teens feel alone and alienated. They see life as meaningless, so they may seek to escape their malaise. Drugs, alcohol, and parties are the most common ways teens cope. I am often asked by parents, "Why do teens use drugs and alcohol?"

My answer: "When teens have a sense of purpose in their lives, it has a calming effect on them. Without it, they become agitated. Teens without purpose and meaning are seeking peace. Remember the acrostic P.E.A.C.E."[14]

> **P**RESSURE—Many teens experience peer pressure to drink or take drugs. Others face internal pressures and feel a sense of relief when they are loaded.
>
> **E**SCAPE—Many teens live pain-filled, stressed-out lives. They want a break. Problems at home, financial worries, adolescent anxieties, and problems with friends cause many to seek escape in drugs and alcohol.
>
> **A**VAILABILITY—Teens tell me that drugs and alcohol are always around. "You can get it anytime, anywhere," they say. A substance-abusing environment surrounds our teens.
>
> **C**URIOSITY—Most teens start drinking or using drugs because they are curious. They wonder what it would feel like to be drunk or high. They wonder whether they might have courage to talk to a "special someone" if they were buzzed.
>
> **E**MPTINESS—Teens who are substance abusers often struggle with feelings of worthlessness and emptiness. Drugs and alcohol temporarily make them forget their pain, but only for awhile.

Pressure, escape, availability, curiosity, and emptiness are five reasons teen abuse substances. Together they spell out what teens are searching for: PEACE.

Top Ten Dangers Teens Face

Entire books have been written about ways teens act out and express their emotions in negative ways (see the Recommended Resources section), so we'll only address the topic briefly. When teens are not experiencing purpose, they may seek to find it in the following destructive ways:

- substance abuse

- sexual activity

- violence or gang activity

- Satanism and the occult

- pornography

- suicide

- eating disorders

- running away

- homosexuality or bisexuality

- escape through media immersion

Surveys indicate that most of these symptoms are increasing among our teens over the last few years. Let's take a closer look at three teen painkillers: substance abuse, sexual activity, and violence or gang activity.

SUBSTANCE ABUSE

More teens are using marijuana now than a decade ago. Over 20 percent of teens report they have used marijuana. This is almost a 100 percent increase over the reported 11 percent in 1988. One-third (32 percent) of older teens (sixteen- and seventeen-year-olds) have smoked marijuana compared to just 14 percent of younger teens. Teen smoking is also on the rise, with 12 percent reporting they have smoked within the last week. The mean age when they started is 12.4 years. Other surveys have found higher proportions of teen smokers than those found by Gallup studies. For example, a survey reported in the *Journal of the American Medical Association* indicated that of some ninety thousand teens in grades seven through twelve, 25 percent consider themselves cigarette smokers.[15]

SEXUAL ACTIVITY

"Since 1991 the number of teens who've had intercourse has dropped from 54 percent to 48 percent, according to the Centers for Disease Control, and teen pregnancy is down slightly as well. Abstinence initiatives are now commonplace around the country."[16] This encouraging finding was reported in *Newsweek*, which also reported that 51 percent of the teens surveyed answered "always" to the question, "Can sexual urges be controlled?" Teens appear to be thinking clearly about the consequences of sex.

VIOLENCE OR GANG ACTIVITY

Parents seem to be more concerned about violence than teens. Teens see it as part of their world. It's the only world they have known; they don't know life without it. Fifty-nine percent of the teens surveyed said they were concerned "a lot" about violence in society. Eighty-two percent of the parents responded the same. When asked the question, "How many teens these days feel a lot of anger. How angry are you?" the chart on the next page tells how teens answered.[17]

These statistics need to be balanced with other Gallup findings that report nearly half of teens say, "There are groups at my school capable of violence, based on what they do, say, or claim they do."[18] Our teens may not be too angry, but they have reason to be afraid— or at least nervous.

How Angry Are You?

Response	Percentage
very	3
somewhat	25
not too	43
not at all	29

In spite of all the coverage on school shootings, school is still perceived as a relatively safe place. A Gallup Youth Survey reports that 60 percent of teens feel that their schools are a place where they feel safe "all the time." Another 35 percent of the teens reported they feel safe "sometimes," leaving only 5 percent who say they "never" feel safe at school.

Purpose at Home

I conclude with the best news. Teens attribute the purpose in their lives to their parents, not their peers. A national, nonprofit organization that works with teens has done extensive research into what makes kids experience a sense of meaning and peace. They have determined that kids need four essentials—safety, love, power, and trust—to experience purpose (which reinforces our findings in the Gallup "Cries of Teens" Survey). In the testing, the index was the highest in reference to teens' relationship with their parents. The group they spend the most time with—their peers—had the lowest ranking as a source of purpose.[19]

As parents we are having an impact. Our teens do want to dialogue with us. They do not want to be left alone to sort things out on their own. It might start out with milk and cookies after school and a casual, "Tell me about your day."

Discussion Questions

PARENT TO PARENT

1. Discuss this statement: "Life loses purpose for those who do not understand their origin or destination."

2. Why are design, destiny, and duty important concepts for teens to comprehend?

3. Discuss the following: "Childhood cannot exist without any adults around. If everybody is equal, then who is in charge?"

4. What relationship does fathering have to developing purpose in teenagers?

5. Do you agree with this statement: "Fathers bring purpose, stability, and resources—characteristics often absent in homes without dads"? Explain your thinking.

TALKING WITH YOUR TEEN

1. What would be an adventure to you?

2. How important is it to your friends to believe that life is meaningful and has a purpose?

3. Use the chart on the next page to discuss the six cosmic questions, the related Scripture verses, and the difference each makes in your life.

4. If your parents were to be more authentic, what would that look like? What impact would that have on your relationship with them?

5. What do you think about the P.E.A.C.E. acrostic? Are there other reasons why teens might get involved with substance abuse?

Six Cosmic Questions

Question	Scripture	So What?
Origin Where did we come from?	Genesis 2:7	God created us. We are supposed to be here.
Design How did God design us?	Psalm 139:3-4	We are created to reflect God's glory.
Morality What has gone wrong?	Romans 3:23	We have not lived up to our created purpose. We have sinned.
Theology How can we fix what has gone wrong?	Romans 6:23	Our sin leads to death, but Christ's forgiveness leads to eternal life.
Duty What should we be doing?	1 Peter 4:10	Serving God (and others) is an expression of our love for Him.
Destiny What lies beyond?	Jeremiah 29:11	God will continue to use us.

Responding to the Cry

THE CRY

The cry for purpose.

THE CHALLENGE

To help our teens develop personal purpose with a sense of adventure, meaning, and intimacy.

TOOLS TO USE AT HOME

1. Get a piece of poster board at least 12 inches by 14 inches and make an adventure poster, contrasting adult adventure with teen adventure. Divide the poster in half and label one side ADULT ADVENTURE and the other side TEEN ADVENTURE. Write descriptions of each or add clippings and photos from magazines, newspapers, and Web sites. Discuss the differences and similarities with your teen.

2. With your teen, discuss the images of fathers he or she has seen in life and through the media.

⚜ Who portrays the best father image on TV?

⚜ Who portrays the best father image in the movies?

⚜ What are the top four characteristics of a good dad?

3. Ask your teen, "If four out of ten children don't have dads in the home, what do you think about a mentoring program?" Explain what mentoring might involve and discuss the idea with your teen. Ask, "Eighty-five percent of teenagers are interested in a mentor of some kind or another. What would you like in a mentor and what would you definitely *not* want?" Make lists that contrast mentors and parents.

4. Choose some activity you can do with your teenager that will force you both to deal with safety, power, love, and trust. It could be something as challenging as rock climbing or white water river rafting—or something equally scary to *you and your teen,* such as ballroom dancing, handcrafts, cooking, or computer classes.

5. Develop some form of artistic expression for the list of six questions on page 105. Make a sculpture, a painting, a poem, a Web page, or use another medium of your choosing.

TOOLS TO USE AT CHURCH

1. Review the last year of sermons or youth group lessons to see if there has been any teaching or practical application offered on achieving purpose. Ask around to see how people might have applied these lessons and ask them if they would be willing to share their story in the youth group.

2. Ask a substance abuse survivor to speak to the youth group on what he or she has learned about pain, purpose, and coping.

3. Research your local community resources and provide parents with contact information for help with the top ten dangers teens face. (See page 123.)

4. Appoint a P.E.A.C.E. task force of adults and teens to brainstorm ways the church can address the reasons teens choose risky behavior. (See page 122.)

5. Provide a lending library for parents of teens. Ask parents to donate books once they have completed them. Ask the church to include a small amount in the annual budget to make books available for parents who may not be able to afford them. Advertise in the church bulletin and other venues. Refer to the Recommended Resources (beginning on page 237) to get you started.

CHAPTER 5

A Cry to Be Heard

Makayla, dressed in nylon warm-ups, folded her arms across her chest and crossed her legs.

"We can't figure out what she wants," confessed her father. "If she had her way, she'd be wearing her headphones now and blaring her music on her Discman."

"She seems to live in a different world," chimed in her mother, Cherise.

The uneasy trio sitting in my office had come for counseling on "how to communicate better."

"Ever since she turned sixteen three months ago and got her license, she seems to be pulling away," Cherise added.

"Makayla, do you have your own car?" I turned my attention to the daughter, who was doing her best to melt into the back of her chair.

"Yeah, I do." She didn't look up as she answered.

"What kind is it?"

"Honda Accord."

"What year?"

"1994."

"Oh, that's a good year. We used to have a '94—in that pretty jade color."

"Really?" Now I had her attention. "That's the same color as mine." She unfolded her arms and put her hands in her lap.

"Do you have a stereo in it—a CD player?" I continued.

"Yeah, Mom and Dad upgraded it for my birthday."

"Are the windows tinted?"

"Yeah," she smiled and raised her eyebrows as she looked over at her parents.

"I can see there's a story here."

All three nodded in agreement.

"What kind of music are you into?"

"All kinds, except for the dinosaur rock *they* listen to," she rolled her eyes as she delivered the punch.

"What was the last CD you bought?"

"Dido."

"Mm-hmm."

"You know Dido?"

"Yes, I like their smooth vocals and harmonies. They're so soothing."

Makayla wrinkled her forehead as she stared back at me, then her eyes darted down to my shoes. She was trying to figure me out. Teens will often check out someone's shoes to see if they are fashionable, cool, or out of it (like their parents).

"Do you run track?" I asked.

"Yeah, how did you know?"

"Your shoes."

She turned red. I had caught her at her own game. "Yeah, I run for West Hills."

"Varsity?"

"Yeah."

"What events?"

"The 400, 200, 4 x 400, and sometimes long jump."

"Which is your favorite?"

"The relay. It's fun working on a team."

"What's your best time this season?"

"We ran 51.1, but our coach thinks we can break 50 with competition."

"That's very good. You'll go to state if you do that."

She smiled. "That's what we're shooting for."

Her parents looked perplexed, so I asked, "Did you know these things about your daughter?"

"Most of it," Anthony responded with a hint of defensiveness.

"But you're really connecting," interjected Cherise. "Why can't we do that?"

"Let's ask Makayla. What's different about how I talked with you today compared to how your parents typically talk with you?"

"They don't listen. They want to talk, but it's more *at* me than *with* me. You really seemed to care, and you were really tuning in to me. You seemed interested in *me*, not just what you wanted to say to me."

"Anything else?"

"You seem to understand and value my world. You didn't try to change it or make it like yours. I felt that you accepted me and what I'm into. I felt like you were really paying attention to me—even checking out my shoes." She looked me in the eye and smiled.

"What would you like from your parents?"

"I would like them to listen to me—I mean really listen. I wish that they would tune in to me and not be so busy and distracted. If we do get into a good conversation, they always work it around to something on their agenda, something I need to do better, like—as they say—watch my attitude or watch my mouth or get better grades or clean up my room."

"Makayla brings up a good point," I said, turning to face her parents. "Do you ever talk to her with the goal of just connecting, rather than correcting?"

"I thought we did, but I guess not," Cherise replied.

"If you try to correct without connecting you end up *disconnect-ing*. Spend some time just getting to know Makayla and what she's thinking. Listen to her heart, her opinions, experiences, and values without evaluating or correcting."

"But what happens if she's doing something wrong?" Cherise asked.

"Is she doing anything wrong now?"

Cherise shook her head. "No. But we just don't feel that close to her."

"Try this. The next time she says something that you want to cor-rect, just let it go. Swallow it. Discipline yourself to remember that not every moment is a teachable moment."

"But isn't it our job to teach her?" Anthony protested.

"Are you able to now?"

"No, not really. She isolates us and lives in her own world."

"Then what you're doing isn't working, right?"

Both parents nodded.

"Then it's time to try something else. When our kids become teenagers, we need to adjust our style of parenting from *control* to *influence*, from director to coach. This means that we don't try to address everything. Can you imagine having a friend who was always correcting your grammar, evaluating your language, and critiquing your decisions? What kind of friend is that?"

"An *ex*-friend!" exclaimed Anthony.

"Exactly. As adults and young adults, like Makayla, we want con-sultation, not critique. That doesn't mean that you bury your head in the sand, but you choose your battles carefully. Otherwise you'll be battling all the time."

"What can we do about her retreating into her music, TV, and computer?"

"Makayla, your parents think you're avoiding them. Is that true?"

"Kinda. I don't want to hear another lecture, but I *would* like to just talk with them."

"Why do you bury yourself in the media—music, MTV, and everything?"

"Because I don't want to get hurt or hassled. Sometimes I just want to talk, but they're so busy or distracted—and it hurts to try, only to be rejected."

"So your parents are, in a way, pulling back from you and retreating into their work, their busy schedules, and other distractions."

"Yeah."

"What distracts your mom?"

"She is so concerned about me being perfect. I think she watches too much afternoon TV about rebellious teens."

"Her distraction might be *worry*?"

"Mm-hmm."

"What about your dad? What distracts him?"

"Work, e-mail, and boring business news on cable."

"So, you don't feel as if you can interrupt your dad, and you try to avoid a lecture or interrogation from your mom."

Makayla smiled and let out a sigh, "That's it."

"So maybe we have a family pattern of retreating, not just a Makayla problem of isolating herself and hiding behind her favorite diversion."

"What can we do?" asked Cherise.

Listening to Your Teen

Like Makayla, teenagers want their parents and other adults to pay attention to them—to really listen. They don't want their needs, ideas, interests, and dreams to be lost in the frantic pace of contemporary life, and they don't want their voices drowned out by the steadily increasing din of technology. They want to be heard. Ninety-one percent of the teens surveyed for the Gallup "Cries of Teens" Survey reported a "very strong" or "strong" need to be listened to. The poll findings affirm that all teenagers, male and female, want their views to be considered and want to be taken seriously.[1]

When we listen to others, we express that we value them. This is the biblical concept of honor. When we listen to others, we communicate that they have worth and are important to us. When something or someone is designated as *honorable,* it means weighty or valuable. A pound of gold is worth more than ten pounds of gravel because of its value. When people feel like they have been heard, they feel appreciated. When we listen, we are sharing ourselves by investing our time and attention in what they are talking about. In a swift-paced world full of sound bites, it is comforting to know that someone will take time to listen to us.

Many teens feel accepted the most when someone sits down with them and takes unhurried time to really listen. Connecting with teenagers means making them feel heard above the noise of our society. It means dealing with the distractions, the media bombardment, and the usual intergenerational misunderstandings. Connecting through active listening requires three essential commitments from parents: a genuine interest, a listening ear, and time.

Do not kid yourself. You need self-discipline, desire, and deliberate action to successfully connect with today's teenagers. Your kids can tell when you are faking it, they know when you are not really listening, and they do not want to be just another item on your schedule. Avoid trying to quickly finesse your relationship with your teenager from a distance. Instead, roll up your sleeves on a daily basis and engage with your teenager.

Here are five key principles to help you listen to your teenager:

- *Eliminate distractions.* Put down the newspaper. Turn off the TV, the CD player, the computer, and the ringer on the phone. If you have to, go someplace where you will not be interrupted so you can talk.

- *Set aside* quantity *time.* When it comes to spending time with your kids, there is no quality without quantity—especially with teenagers, who may need some time just to warm up to what they want to say. When you dedicate time for your teenagers, they not only feel heard but valued.

✤ *Focus on your teen and make an emotional connection.* An emotional connection does not mean that your eyes well up with tears when your child speaks. It means you look beyond the words, the attitudes, and the awkwardness (yours and your teen's) to hear the heart behind what your teenager is trying to say. It means that you ask questions and listen carefully to the answers. Acknowledge your teenager as a distinct individual who is trying out new thoughts, new ideas, and new perspectives. You honor those initial, tentative steps toward adulthood by listening.

✤ *Practice nonjudgmental listening.* Rehearse the following principle until it becomes automatic: Connect first, correct later. When you take time to understand your teenager's thoughts and ideas *before* you weigh in with all your wisdom and experience, you may find that your perspective has changed and the wisdom you have to offer can be applied with even greater discernment and discretion. And when your teenager knows that you're listening, he'll be a lot more willing—and able—to listen to you.

✤ *Be alert to nonverbal communication.* Teens have not developed their verbal skills to the same level as their parents, so they often depend on nonverbal communication—body language, tone of voice, what is left out of the conversation. Tune into these nonverbal cues, which can communicate more than your teen's actual words. For instance, when you ask your son, "How was your day at school?" and he gives you the customary *fine,* take a minute to observe how he is standing. Are his shoulders slumped?

Does he look tired? What kind of tone do you sense in his voice?

Youth seem to know what is best for them and for the nation. Then why aren't we listening to them? Today's teens clearly have the potential to change our society and the world for the better. They have a very special role to play in our new, post-September 11 world. But the nation's spotlight must be on this age group if society is to help them realize their potential. Certainly the stature and health of a nation are directly related to the well-being of its youth.

Our young people are asking questions, and they're not getting answers.

—*Gallup Tuesday Briefing*, 30 July 2002

Be aware of the *deletes* and *detours* that teens offer in their conversations with you. Some of the most important stuff is what they leave out (deletes) or what they want you to think (detours) to keep you from knowing too much. Most of the time deletes and detours are intentional smokescreens, but they just might be a test to see if you are interested enough to interpret the cues as an invitation to get involved.

A few years ago, when my daughter Nicole was in high school, she was telling us about her Friday night plans.

"After the football game, which is at home, we're going to Lamppost for pizza and then over to Chelsea's to watch a video. Is that okay?"

"Who's driving?"

"Zach is. His parents are letting him take their new SUV. It's so cool. It has a hot stereo, leather seats, and room for six. We'll all go together. He doesn't want to drive his car because it's been breaking down lately. Do you know how much it costs to fix a muffler on an old car like that?"

"What time will you be home?"

"How about one?"

"Well, the game is at home and will be over at nine or so. You only need an hour for pizza and two hours for a movie, so we will see you here at midnight."

"Dad, that's hardly enough time to do all that we need to do! Chelsea, Tracy, Carlos, and Zach don't have curfews. Nobody does! Don't you trust me? It's not like I'm going out to drink beer and have sex or do drugs!"

"I do trust you, but I also know that you will have plenty of time to do what you *need* to do."

As it turned out, they did not all go with Zach because he got off work late. Nicole got a ride with Carlos, but she never told us. She also neglected to tell us that the game was not at home but at another nearby school. Because it was somewhere else, they went to another place for pizza, and they did not go to Chelsea's for videos. They went to Mike's and sipped hot cocoa by his fire pit, where they talked until "oops, it's past midnight!"

As you can see, this scenario has a few deletes and detours. It's my opinion that teens sometimes offer deletes and detours to check our interest level. *Do Mom and Dad care enough to ask more questions and get the details?* Teens want to have their cake and eat it too. They want to have their parents tune into them and listen to them, but they don't want it cutting in on their freedom.

Paying Attention

Not only do many parents not listen to their teenagers, an alarming number seem to have adopted a hands-off approach to parenting their adolescents. It's as if they've said, "The kids want to be left alone, so we'll leave them alone." Such an attitude reflects a devastating misunderstanding of the needs of our teenagers.

As individuals on the verge of adulthood, they want a certain degree of freedom, but they don't want to be abandoned. If anything, they're crying out for their parents to break in or invade their world with genuine care and concern. If the adults instead look the other way and focus on their own concerns for success and self-fulfillment, they relegate the next generation to a teen-only world, where they are forced to devise their own rules and look to each other for values and meaning. When teenagers are forced to become a generation unto themselves, they naturally disengage from the adult world.

The problem with this premature autonomy is that adolescents still need their parents to provide guidance, boundaries, and perspective. After all, they're still teenagers, and most lack the necessary wisdom and experience to make wise choices and chart a true course. If this parallel culture is allowed to continue, there's no telling how far afield the next generation will stray.

If we care about our teenagers, we will make the required sacrifices (or investments, to state it in a positive way) to embark upon a cross-cultural journey into this teen-only world.

We will tune in. We will listen. We will seek to understand. We will show them we care. We will help them grow into capable, connected, responsible adults.

Why Listen?

Listening helps us honor and guide our teens and collect useful information for parenting (intelligence for the FBI—the Family Bureau of Investigation). But listening also helps us discover encouragement opportunities. Our teens give us enough material to keep us upset with them 24/7. But if we can listen to them—let them know they are being heard—we will encounter ways we can encourage them. One of the most influential habits we can develop is to listen to our teens and catch them doing, saying, or thinking something commendable and seize the opportunity to encourage them.

Family counselors Norm Wright and Gary Oliver offer some practical advice:

> What is an encouraging environment? It is one in which our kids know they are of value and worth to God and to us. It is one in which we spend more time building and encouraging them than we do scolding and correcting them. It is one in which we honor them by speaking respectfully to them. An encouraging environment is one where our emphasis is on catching them doing good rather than catching them doing bad. We invest more energy in praising them for being responsible than in criticizing and castigating them for falling short of our expectations.[2]

Listen to *lift*. Listen to your teen so you can praise and affirm qualities, decisions, and values that are commendable. The word *praise* literally means to lift up or call attention to. We want to listen to our teens and lift up all that we can about them and encourage them. We become our kids' cheerleaders when we listen to and affirm them.

Listening for Needs

Imagine going to your medical doctor with a sore foot, and he takes one look at you, scribbles something on your chart, and says, "Here, this should work. It's a powerful new pain reliever," thrusts it in your hand, and leaves the examining room.

How would you feel? Like looking for a new doctor.

We expect doctors to take the time to carefully listen to us so that they can make an accurate diagnosis. Sometimes parents are like that harried, inept doctor—they want to prescribe before they diagnose. *It's much more efficient that way,* they reason.

Like doctors, we need to take time to carefully listen to our teens so we can be alert to their needs, to know where it hurts. We cannot have a cookie-cutter approach to teens; we need to listen and assess each individual separately.

> Brothers and sisters, we urge you to warn those who
> are lazy. Encourage those who are timid. Take tender
> care of those who are weak. Be patient with everyone.
> (1 Thessalonians 5:14 NLT)

I like this Scripture because it requires us to tune in to what our teens need. There is not a one-size-fits-all approach to teens.

Note that in some cases a parent will need to *urge* his teen. This comes from the same root word that means to spur a horse. The idea is one of nudging with physical contact. No, I am not advocating that you kick your teenager (although I am sure there are times when you feel like it!). I am advocating a physical presence—picture holding your teen's hand.

For instance, a few weeks ago my daughter Brooke had the opportunity to try out for an elite volleyball club. As it came time for her to go, she became nervous and defiant, "I don't know why you're making me go. I don't want to play club!"

I reached over and grabbed her hand and pulled her up from her refuge of the couch. I went with her to the tryout and stayed the entire time. Sure, she was old enough to go by herself, but I knew this was one of those times that I needed to "urge the idle" and "encourage the timid."

Encourage means to pour courage into someone. There will be times that you listen to your teenager and discover that she needs courage to take on something that frightens her.

When we listen, we may discover our teens are weak and need

our tender care. The idea of help in this context is similar to the paramedic coming alongside someone who has been injured. When our teens have collisions (figuratively and actually), what they need is not a lecture, but a listening ear.

Quick to Listen

In our culture we have put too much emphasis on talking as being the most critical component of communication. We talk, talk, talk and think we are communicating. We assume that communication is the words that we say to someone. The actual words only account for 7 percent of a message. Tone of voice contributes 38 percent and other nonverbal cues such as body language account for 55 percent.[3] In other words, 93 percent of communication is not what we say, but how we say it.

> My dear brothers and sisters, be quick to listen, slow
> to speak, and slow to get angry. (James 1:19 NLT)

Listening can actually reduce anger because we take the time to understand before we speak. Scripture places a premium on listening and tuning into the needs of others. Probably the clearest example is Christ. He took time to express care and respond to the needs of all people. No one was too young or too poor or too disabled or too low-class for Jesus. He took time to embrace the children and look them in the eye and tell them of His Father's kingdom. He knew the importance of physical closeness, touch, time, eye contact, smiling, an open attitude, and clear words. He was the Master Communicator.

Ordinary, common people were important to Jesus—He died for them.

If ordinary people meant that much to Jesus, how much more important should our own teenagers be to us?

Communicate with your teen by emphasizing the nonverbal

aspects of communicating more than the verbal, listening more than talk-ing. Try looking at your teen and smiling. Nod in response, and do not interrupt. If your child makes a mistake with grammar or language, do not correct it—let it go. Correction tends to shut down communication.

Solutions Are Not the Point

We can listen faster than our teens can talk, so what do we do with the extra time? *Think up solutions to their problems or at least refinements to what they are doing.*

What is wrong with this picture?

It's not necessary. We do not need to develop rational responses to our teens' issues. We do not need to make sense of something that does not make sense. When they are talking, our teens do not need our instant, follow-up advice. They do not need us to solve their prob-lems. They need us to listen. During the teen years hormones charge through their bodies and can wreak havoc on their emotions. Emo-tions are not always rational. Sometimes there is not a reasonable explanation for how your teen is feeling.

Here is my recommendation: *You do not have to figure out your teen's emotions. Just listen and try to understand what she is saying.*

"I don't want to take out the trash. I just want to chill and watch TV," responded Nelson to his mother's request.

"Nelson, you're supposed to do it every day, and you've missed some days. It's starting to stink."

"I'll do it as soon as this game is over. I just need a break."

"Why?"

"Nothing."

"Nelson, tell me or you'll be doing another chore in addition to the trash."

"Mom! C'mon."

"Nelson!"

"Oh, all right. School stinks, and I just want to forget about it and watch basketball."

"What happened?"

"Nothing. It's not like I'm failing a class. I just don't like my classes. My teachers are boring and none of my friends are in my classes. I'm stuck with the losers of the school."

"So you really hate school this semester."

"Yeah, it's lame." Nelson looked up at his mom, caught her eye, and then turned back to the game.

"I can see why you wouldn't like to go."

"You can?"

"Sure. It's not fun when you don't see your friends in class and all you have are boring teachers and pointless classes."

He reached for a handful of popcorn, loaded it into his mouth, and then mumbled, "Eggssactleee."

Nelson's mom is wise to not spend too much mental or emotional energy trying to find out or fix the reason he is upset. She just tries to understand. She does not try to fix him.

Being Heard Means Acceptance

Part of hearing our teens is communicating that we accept them as people. If our kids feel that we genuinely accept them and do not secretly wish they were quite different, they will be more likely to respond to our listening. Here are a few questions on acceptance:

- ❖ Do I encourage my teenager to think?

- ❖ Do I communicate to my teenager that she is wrong if she does not agree with me?

- ❖ Do I encourage my teen to discuss controversial subjects with me?

- ❖ Do I affirm my teen for the process of thinking even if he comes to different conclusions than I do?

✤ Do I talk with my teenager when things are going well, or
   do we only talk when my child did something wrong?

Teenagers are very perceptive about our acceptance of them. They
do not focus on the words; they read our nonverbal cues. They are
looking to see if we accept them for who they are—different from us.
When we communicate acceptance of them (not necessarily their
behavior), we are expressing that we hear them and that what they say
matters to us.

I like what a sage youth worker once told me as I struggled with
our teen's autonomy, "If your teen thinks just like you, then one of you
is totally unnecessary."

In my counseling with families, I often see hurried parents who
are too busy to talk with their teens unless there is a problem. I
encourage them to establish a regular habit of talking together—usually over dinner. A routine of talking really pays off when stress and
problems hit the family. It's much easier to learn how to listen when
there is a relaxed, accepting atmosphere. Your teen will not feel heard
and valued if you only talk with him when there is a problem.

When you have developed good looking and listening skills, you
will understand your child better. You will be better equipped to
notice when something is going wrong. When we listen to our kids
and let them empty themselves of negative, painful, and confusing
emotions, they are free to discover some positive feelings and may be
more open to hearing us talk about solutions.[4]

It's easy to look at your teen and get worried. If you are like me,
you think, *There is so much I need to work on!* You might assume that
lectures, intensive confrontation, and brainwashing will do the trick.
But I'm learning that the key to influencing teenagers is relationship.
It's not what you know about communication or adolescence, it's what
you know about *your* teenager. The most effective way to enhance the
relationship and get to know your teenager is to listen to him.

The Art of Listening

A lot of what is written about listening has to do with technique. Maintain eye contact. Lean forward towards the speaker. Affirm by nodding your head. Do not look past the speaker. Repeat and paraphrase what you heard. These skills are important, and they do make a difference. These are aspects of the science of listening. But when it comes to teenagers, listening is more of an art than a science. You can have all of the technique mastered, but if you do not have the heart, it will not matter.

The challenge is to grow a heart for listening. To help you with that, let me offer some self-evaluation questions:

- Do I care about what my teen says?

- Does what my teen says matter to me?

- Am I open to changing my opinion or feelings based on what my teen says?

- Do I want to know what is on my teen's heart?

- Is understanding more important than agreement?

The Influence of the Media

One major obstacle that impedes—and seeks to drown out—the dialogue between parents and teens is the pervasiveness of mass media. Like any technology, the media can be positive or negative. For some teenagers, media provides solace in their teen-only world.

I have noticed that many teens are not comfortable with silence. As soon as they have the opportunity, they turn on the radio, the CD player, or the TV. When teens have free time they like to enjoy the variety of media that is available. Some do it simply for enjoyment, while others do it to escape. Whatever the reason, teens love media.

Ninety percent watch TV every day. Just as likely, they are listening to their CDs (90 percent) or listening to their favorite radio stations (89 percent). Nearly all teenagers are exposed to several forms of media in a twenty-four-hour period. Their usage differs by gender. Boys are more likely to use the Internet (44 percent versus girls at 38 percent) and to play computer games (45 percent versus only 26 percent of girls).

Music drives the pop teen culture. To stay on top of the latest hits, teens need to listen to their favorite radio station every day. It could be social suicide to not know what the latest new song is. As a result, teens may be listening to the radio when they should be doing homework or, if they are like most teens, while they are doing their homework. Parents who have tried to carry on conversations with their teens while music plays in the background know what I am talking about. "Wait! Not now! This is my favorite song." The pervasiveness of the media can infringe on just about any conversation.

Some forms of media may actually help students. There may be a relationship between media consumption and school performance. Teens of above-average standing are more likely to report that they used the Internet (44 percent, compared with students of average or below-average standing).[5] These may be the same students who stonewall their parent's inquiries with, "I can't talk right now. I'm downloading some JPEGs for my chemistry class." The computer might raise the grade, but it also raises a barrier between teen and parent.

Going to the movies is one of the most popular teen pastimes—they go more than once a month (13.6 times a year), about twice the amount the average adult goes. In fact, movies have enjoyed a recent surge of popularity with teens. In 1994 teens went to only eight movies each year.

Twenty-six percent of the girls felt movies are too violent, while only 20 percent of the boys felt this way. Above-average students are also considerably more likely to be concerned about movie violence than teens of average or below-average standing (29 percent of the above-average students versus just 14 percent of other students). Girls were not only more concerned about violence, but they also reported there was too much sex in the movies (34 percent versus the boys at 22 percent). This could indicate a growing fear among girls of being victims of violence or sexual attack. Like a subtle ringing in their ears, the threat of violence can be distracting to girls. Boys tend to think they are immune from such attacks and are not as bothered by sex and violence in the movies.[6]

I share these statistics for two reasons: to help you understand how noisy your teen's world is, and for you to be apprised of what teens think about media. Use this information to launch a discussion with your teen about media. Does it help or hurt?

> The average child spends more than five hours a day with media—and about half that time is watching TV.
>
> —Kaiser Family Foundation

Media as Conversation Starters

If you are a parent of a teenage girl, you may want to discuss with her the portrayal of violence and sex in the movies, TV, and music videos. Many are degrading to women and can make young women feel victimized or objectified. Some forms of media present much more positive roles, but they are rare. Take time to affirm these when you find them. Critique these to see how they cast young women in a favorable light.

For the most part, teens have a positive view of movies. In fact, 70 percent of teens (boys and girls) say that movies have a "very positive" or "somewhat positive" effect on their ethics and morals. However, they take a dimmer view of TV. Just over half (55 percent) say the effect of TV on the ethics and morals of Americans is "very positive" or "somewhat positive."[7]

I agree with the dimmer view of the findings on TV, and I am not as positive regarding the movies. I think teens are more tolerant about movies because it is a chance to get out of the house and away from their parents. Their bias is reflected in the findings.

One evening I was watching TV with Nicole, 21, and Brooke, 18. It was the usual teen fare on one of the newer networks. We watched a popular show, which had the obligatory scene or reference to premarital sex and the newest Hollywood sociopolitical theme, homosexual or lesbian relationships. (The characters were teenagers.) This has become such an overt theme that it has become predictable and boring. It has become a nauseating mantra.

How should a Christian family respond to a culture that is becoming increasingly hostile to our Judeo-Christian foundation? We should respond by using Scripture as our guide and judge for moral truth. In an it's-okay-for-you world, the Bible is like a lighthouse in the relativistic fog. Consider what Peter has to say to our twenty-first-century families.

> Therefore, prepare your minds for action; be self-controlled; set your hope fully on the grace to be given you when Jesus Christ is revealed. As obedient children, do not conform to the evil desires you had when you lived in ignorance. But just as he who called you is holy, so be holy in all you do; for it is written: "Be holy, because I am holy." (1 Peter 1:13-16 NIV)

When our daughters where younger, we simply said no to TV programs that featured nonbiblical themes. Now that they are older, we allow them more freedom for two reasons: their ages (they are both adults) and few TV shows do not offend some biblical principle—except those on Home and Garden TV, which is what my wife and I watch!

The Power of Questions

Now our tack is to prepare our daughters' minds for action. We will watch a TV show and debrief during the commercials. By doing this, we have had some engaging conversations, and we have discovered our daughters' opinions by asking questions and listening to them. We are intentionally trying to create an opportunity for our young adult children to be heard with questions like these:

- How does that scene portray the character who is a Christian?

- Do you think writers of this show have a pro-homosexual agenda?

- How are they supporting or attacking biblical values?

- If you were making this show, how would you do it differently?

These kinds of questions are appropriate for older teenagers, but not for younger ones. You can adapt the choice of shows and your questions to the age of your child and your own family standards. The goal is to train them to think biblically and critically about their choices of entertainment. As a parent, you cannot choose for them. You have to train them to make good decisions. There will come a day when your child is spending the night at a friend's house and will be faced with making a choice regarding entertainment. Have you prepared them for action and to be self-controlled?

A Family Media Covenant

Develop an agreement for family members that promises holy and pure standards in relationship to media. These guidelines will bring

The Smith Family Media Covenant

Flee the evil desires of youth, and pursue righteousness, faith, love and peace, along with those who call on the Lord out of a pure heart.

—2 Timothy 2:22

As a family, we seek to call on our Lord with a pure heart. We promise to avoid anything that is evil and inconsistent with God's Word—in fact, we will flee from it. Instead, we will pursue the following qualities:

Righteousness Making the right decisions
Faith Those things that grow our relationships with God
Love Those things that help us express affection, commitment, and grace to each other
Peace Those things that enhance relationships and resolve conflict

We will not try to do these alone, but we will do them as team members "along with those who call on the Lord." This agreement applies to all that we see and hear, including TV, movies, videos, music, Internet, and print media.

Signature _____ Date _____

Signature _____ Date _____

Signature _____ Date _____

Signature _____ Date _____

unity and strength to your family and will help your teens make tough decisions when they are away from home. Here is a sample.

One of the goals for this book is to help parents obtain an accurate view of what is happening with today's teens, the millennial generation. Looking at what is happening with thousands of teens is likely to help you capture what is going on with your teenager. I commend you for taking the time to understand what is going on inside the world of your teen. If you know the truth about your teen, you are more apt to trust him, but if you are unsure about what is actually happening, you are more likely to be suspicious and distrustful. One way you can enhance the trust in your parent-teen relationship is to find out more about today's teens.

We used to live in a world that did not need media covenants. There used to be agreement about right and wrong. We used to restrict children from exposure to adult situations and material. Now it's an equal-access world. Because of media and technology, children have the same access to material as do adults. There is not a hierarchy of information that delineates media content for children, for teens, or for adults. This is a significant cultural shift. American parents were once expected to raise their children in line with the common cultural views. Today, good parents expect to raise their children in opposition to the culture and most media.

Guidelines for a Noisy World

We live in a world that is clanging with competing messages. In the midst of the racket we need to be able to filter out the distractions and listen to each other. How should parents, youth workers, and teachers respond to this new, media-soaked culture? Here are four guidelines:

- *Learn about new media.* Become familiar with what forms your teen likes and about emerging media technologies. Do not avoid media just because it is new or foreign.

❖ *Ask your teen to help.* Teens today often know far more about technology and media than their elders. Show an interest and ask them to explain or show you around their techno-world.

❖ *Develop clear guidelines for the use of technology.* Monitor recreational and educational use of the Internet. Discuss with your teens rules for safety. For example, "Never use your real name or address with computer contacts unless you know the person." Help them develop strategies to avoid problems while online. Make clear what is acceptable content, use, length of use, and so forth. Some families have found it helpful to have a computer contract, which describes how family members will use the computer: what is acceptable and what is not. Include consequences for broken agreements. For example, the offender may be restricted from using the computer for one week.

❖ *Have a media Sabbath.* Agree to take a break from most forms of media in order to focus on faith, family, relationships, renewal, and rest. This could be one day a month. One family with teens discovered that the first Sunday of the month worked well. They would go to church together, go out to lunch and catch up. They would try not to talk about news or media-related topics. Then they would go home, take naps, and read. At dinner they discussed their books. After dinner they played a table game and had dessert.

Breaking into Their World

Contrary to what many parents believe, our teens do want to have relationships with us. Today's teens trade in relational capital. Their social economy is based on knowing and being known. It is important to them to have a relationship with us, as long as it doesn't interfere with their really important relationships—their friendships!

Notice the absence of the suspicion and alienation of the Generation Gap. With previous generations of teens, parents were likely to be distant from their teens, but millennials aren't pursuing this distance—a gap. They want to connect.

One of the best places to begin is with conversations at home. But what should you talk about? Be willing to take some risk and raise issues you do not normally talk about. Most of us grew up with our parents warning us not to talk about "religion, sex, money, or politics—it's just not polite." Let me encourage you to take the risk of being "impolite" in the privacy of your home. Try talking about these topics, especially if your teen is fourteen or older and impressionable young children are not at the table.

Being Heard Leads to Community

In a fascinating study about the shifts in society, Robert Putnam reports on the loss of community in our country. In his book, *Bowling Alone*, Putnam describes how we used to bowl in leagues, but now we bowl alone. More people are bowling than ever, but leagues are half of what they used to be. We are too busy to be committed to bowling league night. Over recent decades we have witnessed a striking reduction of regular contacts with our friends and neighbors.

We spend less time in conversation over meals, we exchange visits less often, we engage less often in leisure activities that encourage casual social interaction, we spend more time watching (admittedly, some of it in the presence of others) and less time doing. We do not know our neighbors as well, and we do not see our old friends as often.[8]

Millennials long to be on a team. They are more concerned about being connected than being competitive like their boomer parents. Our teens desire to be included. When we respond to their cry to be heard and listened to, they feel included.

"This is a much more team-playing generation," observes William Strauss, coauthor of the book, *The Fourth Turning*. "Boomers may be bowling alone, but Millennials are playing soccer in teams." That makes belonging so crucial that it can be a matter of life and death.[9]

This helps explain the teen clique phenomena. They settle into their gang with its own distinctive tribal markings: hairstyles, clothes, tattoos, body piercing, body painting, shoes, accessories, and music. These are the markers that brand a teen into the group, but that does not mean she will stay there. The youth culture is diverse and changing. That is why it is hard to pin down. It is inaccurate to make conclusions based on the markings. Our attempt in this book is to objectively look at their needs—their cries—not just their distinctive tribal markings.

No one teen incorporates all the attitudes and characteristics that the teachers who teach them, the parents who raise them, the researchers who study them, and the kids themselves, name as the identifying marks of this generation. In large part that is because "today's teens may have less in common with each other than those in generations past," says psychologist William Damon of Stanford University. "Some are absolutely on track: they're bright-eyed, genuine and ambitious. But a significant number are drifting or worse."[10]

Most teens would like more time with their parents. They know they need guides to help them navigate uncertain teen territory. They know their sixteen years of experience does not fully equip them for the challenges they will face, so they are fearful of facing the challenges.

"Adolescents are not a tribe apart because *they* left *us*, as most people assume," says Patricia Hersch, author of the bestseller *A Tribe Apart*. "We left them. This generation of kids has spent more time on their own than any other in recent history."[11]

The parents of millennials are busy with their work and their hobbies. They might have their week organized to spend some time with their teens—to take them shopping or to their activities or out for a bite to eat—but their teens are likely to spend much more time alone.

Data released last year found that teens spend nine percent of their waking hours outside school with friends. Teens spend twenty percent of their waking hours alone.[12]

Millennials may be growing up in a period of prosperity, but they may be lacking a connection with their parents. This explains why they feel such a strong need for community. Relationships are critical. Peers are very important to millennials. They have a hunger to belong and be accepted. They want to be included. Our teens want to be in community to have a voice. They want to be considered valuable enough to be listened to. Our teens want to know that what they say matters to us, because *they* matter to us.

Discussion Questions

PARENT TO PARENT

1. The chapter opens with a scene about Makayla and her family. Who do you most closely relate to—Jenny, her mother, or her father?

2. What are some barriers that you have experienced when you've sought to listen to your teenager?

3. Why does listening express value to a person?

4. What are you doing to make your teens feel heard?

5. Discuss this statement: "You do not have to comprehend your teen's emotions; just listen and try to understand what your teen is saying."

TALKING WITH YOUR TEEN

1. Describe a time when someone *really* listened to you.

2. Use the following material in Connecting with Your Teen to establish a weekly appointment with your teen.

3. "Listening reduces anger because we take the time to understand." Discuss this assertion.

Connecting with Your Teen

Create time to listen to your teen. Schedule a weekly appointment with him or her to discuss these issues. To help get the most of your time together, consider the following tips:

- Schedule a time that is convenient, but unlikely to have conflicts. Many parents report that breakfast time has fewer conflicts. Include food if possible.

- Choose a place that works for your teen. (McDonalds is cheap, fast, and teen-friendly.)

- Let your teen know that you value their input and want it. "I'd like to take you to breakfast and ask you five questions about being a teen. It should only take fifteen minutes. When can we go?"

- Keep it light. Do not expect it to be serious. Be flexible and go with the flow. If your teen does not want to talk too much, move on to the next question or something else. Sometimes they want to talk a lot, and other times they may be quiet.

- Remember the point is to connect with your teen, not to cover the material. Be willing to skip some of the questions.

- Use the Talking with Your Teen questions from each chapter as your guide. You might want to copy them onto a small piece of paper so you do not have to always bring the book.

Parent-Teen Connect Time

Our time to get together is _____

We will meet at: _____ Time: _____

We will try this _____ times

4. Does media influence teens to do bad things? Why do you think that?

5. What are your personal media standards? What changes do you want to make, if any?

Responding to the Cry

THE CRY

The cry to be heard.

THE CHALLENGE

To tune into our teens by listening and eliminating distractions.

TOOLS TO USE AT HOME

1. One day a month have a TV blackout. Encourage reading and a longer dinner conversation.

2. Have dinner together at least three times a week. Do not watch TV, listen to the radio, or answer the phone during the meal. Decide how long (thirty to sixty minutes) you will spend talking over dinner. Protect these times. Play High-Low: Everyone shares the highlight and lowlight of the day.

3. Once a month schedule a family game night. Our family's favorite board game is Cranium.

4. Schedule a reading hour on weeknights. No TV, Internet, or phone calls between 9:00 P.M. and 10:00 P.M. Encourage everyone (including you) to have a fun book to read during this time.

5. Once a month, schedule a two-hour visit to a large bookstore to browse through books and purchase them for your

reading hour. Have family members share books they are interested in while at the store. Sit in a soft chair and read; listen to live music; sip on a café latte. Develop a taste for quieter, less hurried entertainment.

TOOLS TO USE AT CHURCH

1. Start a parents-of-teens group to discuss this book and creative ideas to manage media. One skill parents need assistance with is setting standards for media. For instance, "When should I let my child see a PG-13 movie?" Discussing standards in a group is helpful and practical.

2. Provide contact information for ministries that help parents evaluate and manage media. *Plugged In* by Focus on the Family is an excellent newsletter *(www.family.org/pluggedin)*. Walt Mueller, executive director of the Center for Parent-Youth Understanding, produces a cutting-edge newsletter on media and culture *(www.cpyu.org)*.

3. Develop a newsletter that offers abstracts from these sources for all parents of teens and preteens in your church.

4. One of my favorite seminars is *Understanding Your Teenager* *(www.uyt.com)* developed by Wayne Rice. I think so highly of it, I'm now part of the presentation team that gives the seminar around the country. Sign up for it when it's in your area.

CHAPTER 6

A Cry to Be Valued

She rinsed her mouth a second time with the mouthwash. *I better ask mom to get some more at the store. I'm almost out. I can't run out.*

Karen checked her face in the mirror. She dabbed the towel at the corners of her mouth, drying the small traces of her vomit. *Nobody will find out.* Her stereo blasted from her room, masking any sound of her retching in the bathroom.

Karen has bulimia, an eating disorder. If people knew, they would be surprised. At first glance, she seems to have it all together: good grades, an outgoing personality, a varsity athlete, and a slim figure—one she maintains by making herself regurgitate her lunch every day after school. *No sense in keeping all of those unnecessary calories,* she reasons.

Since eighth grade she has had this compulsion to be perfect—to get the best grades, to be the fastest on the cross-country team, and to be the thinnest of her friends. "After all, you can't be too rich or too thin," she often jokes with her friends.

She has been purging for about two years now. She started during her freshmen year when she gained a few pounds in the off-season between cross-country and track. She tried on a swimsuit at the mall and noticed in the angled mirror that her thighs were a little bigger. She knew that she would be wearing her new swimsuit during spring break. She wanted to quickly lose some weight. Purging seemed to work. She could simply cut back on her eating, keep up her usual workout, purge every day, and see results!

Karen was not from a divorced home. Her parents loved her and had high expectations for her. Both of them had attended college, and they hoped that Karen would be able to attend Stanford or UCLA on a scholarship. Karen was driven to excel. It was not enough for her to be good; she needed to be the best.

It almost killed her.

Karen became obsessed with her weight. She would count the calories of everything she ate. If she went over her allotted amount, she would purge an extra time or run an extra three miles after her two-hour workout with the school team. Her body became rail thin. Her hair was strawlike and dull. Her eyes and cheeks sunk into her skull. She wore a sweatshirt, even when it was eighty degrees outside; she was always cold. After one track workout, she decided she needed to make herself pay for the extra rice cake she'd had at lunch. She left the school and headed out to the hills for her usual three-mile circuit. She became light-headed after the first hill. Before she could catch herself, she fainted. Her face plowed into the jagged rocks on the trail.

Fortunately, this trail was popular with mountain bikers. Within a few minutes one rider came along and discovered Karen sprawled across the trail. He jumped off his bike and tried to revive her. She was breathing, so he didn't give her CPR. He poured water from his water bottle over her head. It revived her. He held her head with one hand and fed her the rest of the water from his bottle. His buddy arrived and called 9-1-1 on his cell phone. He also retrieved a Power Bar from his saddle pack and gave it to Karen.

Karen munched on the bar, thankful to be discovered by the two mountain bikers. If it wasn't for them, she could have spent the night alone in the wilderness. The pounding in her head subsided after she drank the water and ate the nutrition bar. She was too weak to walk, and the cuts on her face stung with dried sweat. As she sat there, waiting for the paramedics, she thought, *I wonder how many calories were in that Power Bar?*

A Cry for Approval

Karen almost died trying to get her parents' attention and approval. "All I wanted them to say was, 'That's good.' Instead, I got, 'Try a little harder.' It was never enough. I wasn't thin enough, smart enough, fast enough, pretty enough, or happy enough. I didn't measure up. Even when I did my best, they didn't notice."

In Karen's case it was a cry for approval, but for most of America's teens it's beyond that. It's a *cry to be valued.* This is the cry to be appreciated, the longing to be considered more important than other things and most other relationships in a parent's life. The cry to be valued can be defined as *the need to be considered as having a high degree of worth and importance.*

When we think of worth, we are often talking about objects. *Webster's Dictionary* describes it as "that quality of a thing according to which it is thought of as being more or less desirable, useful, estimable, important, etc."[1] It is the worth or the degree of worth evaluated against a scale or standard.

Applying this concept to teenagers means that we see an inherent quality within them in spite of their behavior, grades, personality, or levels of responsibility. It means communicating to them, "I value you regardless of how you perform."

Akin to love, unconditional acceptance sends a huge message to our teens. *You mean very much to me. You matter to me. There is nothing you can do to lose your worth to me.* In the topsy-turvy teenage world, the solace of unconditional acceptance provides a safe harbor for the teen who may ask himself twenty times a day, *Am I worth anything to anybody?*

The second element of the cry to be valued is importance. Our teens wonder, *Where do I fit in my parent's priorities? Do I come before their jobs? After their hobbies? After their favorite TV show? Where do I rank on my parent's top ten?*

To be considered important is to be considered significant or noteworthy. If a person is important to us, we will not overlook him, ignore him, or demean him. We will treat him with respect and attention.

Important also means to be ranked in a high position. This does not mean that we treat our teenage children like celebrities or let our lives revolve around them, but it does mean that we consider their needs, thoughts, feelings, and opinions. We consider these important to us because they are important to our teens.

> Do nothing out of selfish ambition or vain conceit, but
> in humility consider others better than yourselves.
> (Philippians 2:3 NIV)

It is a biblical approach to consider others important and valuable, especially our teenage sons and daughters.

In our Gallup "Cries of Teens" Survey, the findings report that 88 percent of the teens surveyed responded that being appreciated or valued was a "very strong" or "strong" need in life. The third response of "somewhat of a need" garnered only 6 percent. This indicates that nearly nine out of ten teens regard being valued or appreciated as essential. In other words, if they sense they need it, they *really* need it.

This is particularly true of females, aged sixteen and seventeen. Ninety-four percent of these young women report that being valued is a "very strong" or "strong" need in their lives.

This is notably higher than the 88 percent response of all teens. Why do young women want to be appreciated and valued?

Because God made them that way.

What if? What if those deep desires in our hearts are telling us the truth, revealing to us the life we are *meant* to live? God gave us eyes so that we might see; He gave us ears that we might hear; He gave us wills that we might choose; He gave us hearts that we might *live*. The way we handle the heart is everything. A man must *know* he is powerful; he must *know* he has what it takes. A woman must *know* she is beautiful; she must *know* she is worth fighting for.[2]

Our young women want to know that they are worth fighting for. They want to be pursued and included on a noble quest. They want to be prized and cherished as objects of our affection.

When our daughters were younger, they loved to try on their new Sunday-best dresses. My wife, Suzanne, is an excellent seamstress and would make extraordinary outfits for Nicole and Brooke. They would fix their hair in a special 'do and experiment with lipstick, shoes, and tights. Then there would be an unveiling. As I sat comfortably on the couch, they would enter the room to much fanfare and lively music. They would proudly waltz in like they were on a New York fashion walkway and twirl around in their flowing dresses. Their eyes never left mine. *Does Daddy think I'm pretty? Does he notice me? Am I worth looking at, more than the game on TV?*

Our teens, particularly our girls, wonder if they are valuable to us.

Paying Attention

"Nobody is paying attention to individual adolescents, but everyone is hysterical about the aggregate. Just utter the word 'adolescent,' and all anybody talks about are problems," writes Patricia Hersch in her book *A Tribe Apart.* She also summarizes the findings from the Carnegie Council on Adolescent Development. "In other words, *half* of all of America's adolescents are at some risk for serious problems like substance abuse; early, unprotected sexual intercourse; dangerous accident-prone lifestyles; delinquent behavior; and dropping out of school. The report concluded that today's children are susceptible to a 'vortex of new risks . . . almost unknown to their parents or grandparents.'"[3]

The risks are unknown to us because we are not paying attention. We do not know our own teenagers. We only know them as a group, and they frighten us. Our own teenagers have become strangers. As Patricia Hersch says, they are "a tribe apart." They have not left us; we have left them. We have a generation of abandoned teens. They might have the latest Sony PlayStation, the trendiest shoes and jeans, and the top CD blasting in their headphones, but they do not have us.

"A clear picture of adolescents, of even our own children, eludes us—not necessarily because they are rebelling or avoiding or evading us. *It is because we are not there.* Not just parents, but any adults. American society has left its children behind as the cost of progress in the workplace . . . adolescents are growing up with no adults around, a deficit of attention, and no discussion about whether it matters at all."[4] With all of the school shootings, people are quick to blame the shooters as whacked-out weirdos with a grudge. It is a subtle way of blaming all adolescents. Instead of discovering what is going on in the life of the individual, we dismiss them as being part of a troubled generation. We categorize, stereotype, and dismiss in one quick judgment. As a result, they experience a lot of anger.

A *Newsweek* article reported that "today's teens are the most occupationally and educationally ambitious generation ever. . . . Regardless of what their terrified parents suspect, the belief that today's teens 'are more sexual, rebellious, and inebriated is flat-out wrong,' says pediatrician Victor Strasburger of the University of New Mexico. In 1997, 48 percent of high school students had had sexual intercourse, compared with 54 percent in 1991, according to the Center for Disease Control in Atlanta."[5]

When we stereotype teens, we reinforce our prejudice. When we categorize them into one clump, we devalue them. But when we pay attention and listen to them, we begin to see them as individuals, each with their own stories.

That is all that Karen (from our opening story in this chapter) needed—someone to pay attention and to show she was valued by coming to know her story. Karen did not have problems because she was rebellious; she struggled because she felt alone.

Being Alone

The most remarkable change for teens today is their aloneness. The adolescents of the 1990s were more isolated and unsupervised than previous generations. The teens of the new millennium are even more alone. Teens used to have to devise ways to get away from adults; now they often devise ways to be with them. Millennial families feature Mom at work. The neighbors are strangers, and relatives live out of state. The teenager has several hours of unsupervised time after school with access to a bed, alcohol, a car, and in most homes, a gun. Most parents of teens worry about their kids going out at night, when they should be worried about what they are up to after school. With the cumulative experience of friends, it does not add up to making good decisions. Today teens can easily do more good or bad without any adults knowing about it. One afternoon can destroy a teen's life.

Not only have adults become separated from their own children, says sociologist Dale Blyth of the Search Institute, "Even more importantly, they have gotten separated from the other children in the community. As that happens you have less and less people who might see something to be concerned about, to talk about, and less ability to act collectively to do something about it." It is a problem not just for families but also for communities when the generations get so separated. The effects go beyond issues of rules and discipline to the idea exchanges between generations that do not occur, the conversations not held, the guidance and role modeling not taking place, the wisdom and traditions no longer filtering down inevitably. How can kids imitate and learn from adults if they never talk to them?[6]

It used to be that teens were partially raised by the community. If an adult saw a teen spraying paint on a park bench, he might tell him to stop. Now, most adults would be too afraid to confront a "tagger," fearing that he might be attached to a gang and react with violence. There are fewer people paying attention to teens. There are fewer eyes to notice and fewer ears to listen. It does take a village to raise a teenager, but all of the villagers seem to be at work. As a result, many teens are left on their own to make decisions about substance abuse, sexual activity, media, violence, and friends. When they make poor choices, the adult villagers let them have it when they get home. *What's wrong with kids these days?*

Our culture is suffering from a huge disconnect. We are spending significantly less time with friends and neighbors than we used to. It could be that we have shifted our time allocated for social encounters to time alone at the health club or in our home exercise rooms or at the bowling alley.

Virtually alone among major sports, bowling has come close to holding its own in recent years. It is the most popular competitive sport in America. Bowlers outnumber joggers, golfers, or softball players more than two to one, soccer players (including kids) by more than three to one, and tennis players or skiers by four to one. . . . Unlike health clubs, bicycling, jogging, exercise, swimming, tennis, golf, softball, and all other major sports, bowling is solidly middle-American: common among both men and women, couples and singles, working-class and middle-class, young and old. Given population growth, more Americans are bowling than ever before, but *league* bowling has plummeted in the last ten to fifteen years. Between 1980 and 1993 the total number of bowlers in America increased by 10 percent, while league bowling decreased by more than 40 percent.[7] We are too busy to make a commitment to a weekly bowling league. We simply do not have the time we used to, to make connections.

Parents are not connected with their teens. Adults are disconnected from neighbors and other parents. Teens are not connected with adults in the community. This lack of community has caused teens to feel devalued and forgotten.

"My dad spends more time with his caddy than he does me,"

confided one fifteen-year-old boy who happens to love golf and would love to golf with his dad.

"My mom goes to the health club every day for two hours, but she never has the time to take me shopping or even out for a smoothie," said a thirteen-year-old girl.

"My parents are really into the Internet. They both work all day, and then they get home and play around on their computers until my bedtime. About the only time we have to talk is over dinner, but the TV is usually on, and it's not even a sitcom. It's usually CNN," explained a sixteen-year-old boy.

How can teens learn from their parents if they never talk with them?

Consider the ramifications of parents abdicating responsibility for teaching morals to their teens. Seizing the teachable moments and illustrating with stories and consequences, a parent can have layers of daily interaction with their teens. But if they are not available or are emotionally tuned out, they are contributing to the creation of an immoral teenager. A parent may feed and clothe his teenager, buy him expensive toys, enroll him in lessons and sports, but if he fails to pass on a sense of right and wrong, he is guilty of moral neglect. A generation that genuinely cares for its children would instill morality from the preschool years on and would not back off even during adolescence when they challenge the rules. It may be unpopular to demand certain ethical standards of teenagers, but it is necessary.

But the current generation of parents generally does not seem that interested in going to all the trouble to have such conversations about morals with their teens. It is so much easier to give in and hand teens prophylactics. Teaching chastity takes time, and who has time these days?

The Hurried Teenager

David Elkind coined the term *the hurried child* in 1981, about the year the first millennials were born. Millennials have been hurried their entire lives. Since their early days, millennials have been carted around in minivans by their parents, who were seeking to give them every enrichment opportunity available: gymnastics, prekindergarten, Gymboree classes, play groups, dance, soccer, karate, Little League, hockey, skating, art classes, and Scouts—all before they reached the ripe old age of eight.

The hurried child is not necessarily a happier or more competent child. Too often, the hurried child becomes a stressed child. When parents hurry children, it's usually a result of parents pushing to succeed or because their own lives are so hurried.

By the 1960s, parents could assign just about every aspect of their kids' intellectual and moral development to institutions—schools, day cares, churches, tutors, enrichment classes—as they refocused their energies into self-fulfillment and earning money. For those on the fast track to career and material success, raising children can now be a compelling hobby rather than an occupation. Support institutions cover the child's hours from 7 A.M. to 7 P.M. so that elite parents can turn their type A personalities to enrichment in the evenings.[8]

Busy parents want to give their children the most advantages—the competitive edge. It is not enough for these children to be normal; they need to be above average. In some ways they become symbols of their parents: my son the all-star soccer player, our daughter the star ballerina. The parents' zeal to produce superkids is a way of masking the guilt they have for leaving them. They reason, *If I can't be with them, I'll buy them opportunities.* This behavior often increases during the teen years. Parents sense that their middle school child is seeking to pull away and become his own individual. They reason that their teens want to be left alone. So at a time when their teens need them the most, their parents pull back from guidance, nurture, and connection. In the interest in helping them, they have abandoned them.

Consider what talk-show host Michael Medved and his wife, Diane, a psychologist, write:

But the one thing parents rue is that they *just do not have the time*; they hurry their children because *they are hurried themselves*. Because they've bought the idea that having it all is a worthwhile goal for themselves, tragically, they destroy childhood by pushing their young children to have it all as well. Adults squeeze all of life's facets—marriage, career, working out, church, friendships, relaxing with TV, and parenting—into the day. If we see childhood as a time for special nurturing and exploration, we should be protecting our children from the encroachment of too many activities rather than dragging them along into our pursuit of them.[9]

Moving Targets

Perhaps one of the best things we could do for our children would be to slow down—our lives and theirs—and spend time together. Focus more on connecting and less on competition. Most parents assume they are helping their children by enhancing their lives with activities, but too much can be counterproductive. We need to allow children time to be children. We need to allow teens time to be teens. We do not need to always rush our kids into the next stage of life. Parents on the achievement treadmill are focused on the future, not the present. *You must get into a good preschool to get the basics that will help you become an early reader. You must get into the accelerated track in elementary school to help you test well in your middle school years. These tests will determine whether you make it into honors in high school. If you do well, you can take advanced placement courses and get college credit during high school. Mix in a few SAT prep classes and you'll earn yourself a good score and entrance into a fine university, which enables you to get a well-paying job. Then you can buy lots of stuff and start the cycle again with your kids.*

Parents need to support and encourage their teens, but when they push, they teach an incomplete message: *Success is achievement.* Genuine success is more than a high GPA from a good school. Success is mastering virtues that help one handle success. It is helping teens develop integrity, reliability, compassion, honesty, and charity. Parents would benefit their teens more if they emphasized character as much as competency and a sense of pace rather than haste.

Our teens need us in spite of their groans and their rolled eyes. They do not want to be left alone.

All adolescents are ultimately alone in their search for identity, whether at the top of a mountain or in a crowded room, flopped on their bed listening to music alone, or strolling the mall in a pack. It cannot be forgotten that the self-conscious journey inevitably also occurs *in a context*. Today's teens have grown up in the midst of enormous social changes that have shaped, reshaped, distorted, and sometimes decimated the basic parameters for healthy development. They have grown up with parents who are still seeking answers about what it means to be an adult man or woman. They have lived in families that seldom coincide with the old ideal, and in a culture where the traditional wisdom of how to raise children has been replaced by a kind of daily improvisation as parents try to fit child rearing into their busy lives. At a time when adolescents need to emulate role models, the adults around them are moving targets. Nobody seems to know what normal is anymore.[10]

Rites of Passage

Teens live in a rapidly changing world. They are looking for cues about what is normal and healthy. The adults in their world may be a blur of activity as they do their drive-by mentoring. Our teens need rites of passage—formalized thresholds that announce their arrival at certain developmental stages and their progress through life. They need to know what is important and what they should be working on.

In an observant Jewish family, preteens look forward to their Bat Mitzvah or Bar Mitzvah. They spend years in religious training, memorizing large portions of the Torah and learning about the Jewish faith, history, and culture. Then they join their parents in planning the celebration of becoming a man or woman of the Torah.

We need similar rites of passage in our Christian tradition, to prepare our sons and daughters for adolescence. We need to ground them as men and women of God's Word. Too few church-sanctioned rites mark a teenager's journey toward adulthood. In a rite of passage, a teen discovers meaning and his place in the adult faith community. He learns that he is a valuable member of the family of God and has something to contribute.

When does a boy become a man in our society?

- Is it when he's old enough to drive?

- Is it when he's eligible for military service?

- Is it when he can buy his own beer?

- Is it when he has sex with a woman?

And what about a girl? When does a girl become a woman? She, too, faces social and physical markers. When does she become a woman?

- Is it as soon as she begins her menstrual cycle?

- Is it when she gets married?

- Is it when she gives birth to her first child?

These are *events*, not passages. *Passage* implies a journey in which there is a destination, a plan on how to get there, and significant lessons to learn along the way. Spiritual milestones, true passages, define the journey from childhood to adulthood, offering parents the opportunity to teach lessons from those who have gone before, provide a clear vision of the destination of godly adulthood, provide a plan on how to get there through godly disciplines, and form mentoring relationships for ongoing accountability. Each child must understand that the passage from childhood to adulthood is more spiritual than physical. And there is a wonderful reason for striving to reach the destination: to honor and serve God, which is true purpose in life.[11]

Our teens have lost more than secure families and adult interaction; they grow up in a world that lacks consistency and structure. There is an overwhelming menu of lifestyle choices for our teens. At the same time, their homes and communities fail to provide stability and a place to belong. We have provided a world with many options for our teens, but we haven't given them the skills to select among the options. A rite of passage helps teens focus; it demonstrates that a few things are very important. It serves as a North Star for the teen as he navigates the waters of adolescence.

Pamela Erwin writes about the need to celebrate rites of passage. "In many cultures, life changes such as puberty, marriage, and the birth of the first child, are celebrated with great fanfare. In our contemporary American culture, however, we have lost the sense of passion and celebration for many of the transitions in our lives. With the loss of rites-of-passage rituals in our culture, adolescents have established their own rituals such as getting tattoos and body piercings."[12]

The Blessing

One of the powerful rites of passage is to pass on a blessing to one's teenager. In studying Genesis 27, I discovered that a blessing could have an incredible impact on a child, just like a lack of blessing can leave a child wanting.

At my church we have developed a blessing retreat designed for children eleven to fifteen years old and their parents, which teaches parents to bless their children and kids to honor their parents. At the end of the weekend, we ask the parents to stand in a circle with their children in a circle in front of them. The parents have their right hands on their children and their left hands on the shoulders of the parents to their left in what we call the Circle of Affirmation.

"Each of you sons and daughters have received your parent's blessing today," I explain. "I hope you will never forget the promises and affirmations made to you today. Now, we as your parents want to affirm that we no longer see you as children; we see you as brothers and sisters in Christ. You are joint heirs with us. We welcome you to the family of God and affirm that you are a valuable member. We need you. We bless you in the name of Jesus."

Usually at this time there are a few sniffles. I have had some teens tell me, "No one has ever said that I was valuable or that they needed me. Today I feel blessed, not simply by what my dad said, but by what happened in that circle."

We ask the parents to affirm their teens publicly. Parents are able to say what they have never said before:

"I want my son to know I am proud of him."

"I am so proud of my daughter. She is really becoming a beautiful woman of God."

"My son doesn't live with me, so this time is very unique and valuable. That is what I think of him—he is unique and valuable."

The parents have given small gifts and made custom promises of commitment to their children. It always makes a huge impact. It might be a simple river rock with the teen's name and a Scripture verse written on it with a Magic Marker, but it becomes a family heirloom.

Next, the teens honor their parents. As they stand in the circle, they can see the impact that the words of affirmation have on other teens and parents. Even the most hard-hearted and cold teen softens up at this point.

"Uh . . . I want to say my dad's cool. Not too many guys would spend the weekend with their kid like this. But I am glad mine does. I look up to him."

The boy's dad was amazed when he heard these favorable words from his fifteen-year-old son. "All I have heard for weeks are complaints and grunts. This was really refreshing—actually surprising!"

One fourteen-year-old girl said, "My mom is a single mom and works really hard to make our family work. She makes time for me, even with her busy schedule. I want to honor her. I am proud to be her daughter. When I grow up, I hope I have half of her strength and love."

By this time her mother was a puddle of tears. They embraced and cried joyfully for a few minutes, then turned to listen to another teen who was obviously struggling to speak.

"My dad almost didn't come . . . you may not know it, but he's real sick. He has cancer. I know he wanted to come on this retreat to pass on a blessing to me—his only daughter. But we almost stayed home because he was too weak. This meant so much to me that he came, even though he would rather be in bed. I do not know how much time we will have together. It might be years, or it may only be days. But I want to tell everyone that I know my dad loves me. But even more important than that is that he loves Jesus. As we face death, it's this fact that keeps us going. I am proud of you, Daddy. I love you. I honor you because of who you are."

There was hardly a dry eye in the circle.

Each teen affirmed his parent in some way. It's a small miracle to get teens to publicly affirm their parents. My church has done this retreat with hundreds of parents and teens. It is one of the most influential ministries we have encountered.

Why?

It makes teens feel valuable. It makes parents declare their love and commitment to their teens.

We also offer a rite of passage for graduating seniors. We have a worship time, and then I instruct the parents and seniors on the five points of a biblical blessing.

BOND PHYSICALLY—We need to express appropriate affection to our teens.

LIFELONG FRIENDSHIP—Our teens need to know that we like them and will be there for them.

ESTEEM HIGHLY—Our teens need to know we value them.

SPOKEN WORD—We need to speak words of affirmation and encouragement to our teens.

SPECIAL FUTURE—We need to picture a future of significance, hope, and faith.

For the Senior Blessing, we begin the evening with refreshments and conversation time with the seniors, their parents, and our youth ministry team. It is an unhurried time for us adults to express appreciation for the seniors and their value to us. Our goal is to make everyone feel honored. We want to honor the seniors for their academic accomplishment. We want to honor the parents for their support of their teens' academic achievement and their help keeping their teens plugged into the youth group. We want to honor the youth staff that volunteer their time to minister to the students. Our purpose is to create an atmosphere of mutual honor.

We then focus on honoring the Lord through worship. The student band leads us. For many parents, this is their first exposure to our youth group. The worship may be foreign to them, but they are showing they value their sons and daughters by participating.

Then I present a short talk on the importance of rites of passage:

❖ They mark progress on the journey.

❖ They affirm effort, investment, and growth.

❖ They introduce youth to new levels of responsibility and freedom.

❖ They create an intergenerational experience.

✛ They help us connect as a community—a family of families.

✛ They build memories and help us pass on values through stories.

✛ They help us integrate God into our life stages.

I also review how empty we feel if we never receive our parents' blessings but how empowered we feel when we do.

"Now it is time for you parents to pass on your blessing to your graduating seniors," I announce. "Use the sheets that we have handed you and take a few minutes to write down what you want to say for each of the five parts of the blessing. The seniors will join our youth ministry team at the back for some refreshments. After a few minutes, they'll rejoin you at your table, and you'll have twenty minutes to affirm your teen by giving a biblical blessing patterned after Isaac's in Genesis 27."

Some of the parents stare at the ceiling tiles with blank looks on their faces. They have never done anything like this. Eventually, they settle in and creativity kicks in. When the seniors return to their parents, some sit at tables, while others move to a quiet corner in the room.

One year Mark sat in a corner with his mother and father who had been divorced for about a year. Mark told me later, "It was the first time I was alone with my mom and dad in years. They didn't fight or give each other mean looks. They just focused on me and gave me their blessings." He wiped a tear from his eye.

When they finished giving Mark their blessings, his mom and dad shed tears too. They hugged Mark and then waited in silence.

"It was kind of awkward, because other parents were going on and on, but mine weren't saying a thing. But it was okay. Just sitting there, together, in silence made me feel like they cared. It made me feel like I was worth something. I hadn't felt that in years."

Our teens need monuments—symbolic reminders and celebrations as they reach key points of their development. I believe this strongly enough to have written a book on *Family Traditions: Practical, Intentional Ways to Strengthen Your Family Identity*. In it, my coauthor, Otis Ledbetter, and I write this:

> **Principle:** Milestones in the life of a child are important and should be marked with significant ceremony or commemoration.
>
> **Intentional Impact:** We will establish rites of passage in the life of our children representing freedom of choice coupled with adult accountability. . . . Growth lines create clear visual markers for a child to remember. Taking into consideration *spiritual, emotional,* and *social* aspects of life, milestones will occur at differing intervals. There comes a time in every child's life when the interval between adolescence and spiritual adulthood must be bridged. The connection should be remembered by placing a symbolic monument in her life, a mark on her spiritual doorjamb to remind the child that it's OK to become an adult. It serves to prompt her to take responsibility for her own decisions and actions as a spiritual grown-up.[13]

Suggested Rites of Passage

Some key times to build monuments and celebrate with a rite of passage are

- when your child accepts Christ
- First Communion
- baptism

⚜ graduating from elementary school

⚜ preparing for the adolescence weekend

⚜ graduating from middle school

⚜ at the time a vow of chastity is made

⚜ parental blessing

⚜ Christian Bat Mitzvah or Bar Mitzvah

⚜ sixteenth birthday

⚜ high school graduation

⚜ college graduation

⚜ engagement

⚜ marriage

If we can affirm our children at these key moments, they will feel loved and valued. But it won't happen by accident. We have to be intentional and take initiative. A helpful resource for planning rites of passage is *Spiritual Milestones,* published by Focus on the Family's Heritage Builders' ministry and written by Jim and Janet Weidmann and Otis and Gail Ledbetter—four of my friends who have expressed the value of their children through regular celebrations of spiritual passages. All three of these books are specifically written to address the cry to be valued.

Consider what the authors have written in *Spiritual Milestones:*

> Do you set aside time to pray for your teen? Some parents find it helpful to fast and pray for their kids at least one day per week. We can help our teens see the power of prayer when we ask them every week what we can pray for them. They may be concerned about

a tough exam or a friendship that's run aground. They might even talk about a particular temptation they're facing. At the end of the week, remember to tell your teen you were praying for him or her. Together, you will see how God answers your prayers. Hold each other before God, and let it be a pleasure to pray for one another.[14]

School Prayer

Brooke was showing signs of stress, so I asked her, "What's stressing you out?"

"School. Too much homework—all due at the same time, and it's just too much!"

Since I knew her classes were beyond my capability to help her, I offered, "I will pray for you." That night I tucked her into bed and we prayed that she would sleep well and experience peace and relief from anxiety as she prepared for her oral report, one of five huge projects. I kissed our seventeen-year-old goodnight and assured her, "I'm sure God will help you relax, prepare, and do well." The next morning I promised to pray for her during her presentation.

When she got home that night, she asked, "Dad, did you pray for me today?"

"Yes, I did, at eleven, right when you were supposed to present."

"Thanks. It worked! You know I presented with Mal—it was our oral report. So I asked her to pray with me in class, right before we presented. She looked at me kind of strangely and then said, 'Sure. Let's do it.' She prays and all, but I don't think she's thought much about praying for school stuff, let alone, praying while she's *at* school. Anyway, it helped! We did great. It went really well. Thanks for praying." And she was off.

Spiritual milestones begin with small investments like praying with your teenagers. Do not worry about designing elaborate rites of passage events. Start simply with routines you can lay the foundation with—like expressing how you value your son or daughter by talking to God with them.

Challenge to Churches and Parents

George Gallup Jr. has been a leader in polling our youth and addressing the issues discovered in the Gallup Youth Survey. He challenges parents and church leaders with his words:

> The American school environment is being polluted by violent groups, as reported in recent issues of *YouthViews*. Much of the burden for changing this youth culture from a dangerous to a peaceful one falls on faith communities, since half of teens attend religious services every week. Yet only 13 percent of teens say people their age are influenced a "great deal" by religion, indicating that the impact of churches is not very deep. The rest say teens rely on themselves, opening the door to the authority of violent groups and cults. Youth programs in many churches and other faith communities are, with glorious exceptions, faltering or non-existent. Yet they are desperately needed. Many teens live in a world of fear and uncertainty. So one cannot exaggerate the importance of paying close attention to the spiritual life in schools, churches and the home. Youngsters with a sincere and healthy faith dimension in their lives tend to be happier and better adjusted to life than their counterparts, as well as more likely to do well in school, and more apt to keep out of trouble.
>
> To fail to give young people full attention at this

time of profound spiritual need is to store up problems for generations to come.[15]

As a Fellow with The George H. Gallup International Institute, I
have the privilege of attending the Ideas for Progress seminars.
Recently, the topic was "Youth on the Edge: What's Beneath the
Violence?" One afternoon we had a panel discussion with experts on
youth violence in the schools. Included were two administrators
from Jefferson County Schools, Colorado—the school district of
Columbine High School. We were encouraged to ask questions of the
panelists.

"Did Columbine have any self-esteem programs? All the reports
seem to indicate that Dylan and Eric struggled with being accepted
and were lashing out because of low self-esteem."

"Yes," responded Betsy, one of the administrators. "We had a
rather intensive confidence program at Columbine, as we do at all of
our high schools."

"Well, why weren't they discovered? Did you have an intervention
program?"

"Certainly we did. We had a very comprehensive intervention
program. It was based on peer student training, counseling, referrals,
and support from our district, social services, the sheriff's department,
and the probation department. It was very well developed."

"How about anger management programs? Anything along those
lines?"

Betsy stayed cool and responded to the challenging questions,
"Yes, we had an anger management program as well as an antihate
campaign and systems to deal with alleged hazing and sexual harass-
ment cases." She paused to sip her water before continuing, "Let me
paint a picture for you. Jefferson County School District has eighteen
high schools. Columbine is only one of the eighteen. In some ways, it
is our premier high school. It had all of the self-esteem programs; it
had all of the intervention and anger management programs. You've

seen the facilities on TV and know that we had state-of-the-art facilities and cream-of-the-crop teachers. We had ten different programs in place that Dylan and Eric could have benefited from, but they didn't."

Someone articulated our thoughts. "Well, what happened? How did they fall through the cracks?"

Betsy straightened herself in her chair. She scanned the crowd, establishing eye contact, and gathered our full attention, "You are asking me, 'Why did the shootings at Columbine happen?' It's not an issue of school programs, facilities, security, or parental responsibility. It's a sickness of the soul. Frankly, we were surprised at just how *evil* Dylan and Eric were."

Somehow, everyone in the room knew exactly what she was talking about, and we agreed. There was a moment of silence as we reflected on her words *sickness of the soul.* Her words reminded me of a familiar verse:

> The heart is deceitful above all things and beyond cure. Who can understand it? (Jeremiah 17:9 NIV)

Choosing a Blessing or a Cursing

When teens don't feel valued, they are more likely to seek power through undesirable behavior. We can help them by enhancing their perspectives of themselves as valuable members of the community, school, and home. But our teens need more than a self-esteem program at school; they need parents who affirm them and help them develop a sense of personal value. It takes time and focus to do this, but we can make it a natural part of our daily family life. As I see it, every day we have the choice to offer our young people a cursing or a blessing. I choose the blessing.

> I, the LORD your God, am a jealous God, punishing the children for the sin of the fathers to the third or fourth

> generation of those who hate me, but showing love
> to a thousand generations of those who love me and
> keep my commandments. (Deuteronomy 5:9-10 NIV)

Each generation passes on its dysfunction, sin, and quirkiness to the next generation. According to Deuteronomy 5, the consequence of hating God has a negative impact on children and grandchildren. God's principles are absolute, and those who defy Him and His ways are bound for trouble.

But if we love God, embrace His commandments, and teach these to our children and grandchildren, we experience His blessing for a thousand generations! We bless our teens when we value them. We bless our teens when we show them they have a high degree of worth. We bless them when we convey our appreciation to them. We bless them when we pray for them and ask God to guide their lives and give them a heart for Him. We bless them when we model our passion for God to them.

Tom's Interruption

One Sunday I taught our middle school group on growing a passion for God. I talked about how being a Christian is more than being nice. Being a passionate Christian means being on an adventurous journey, filled with battles to fight, people to rescue, and a cause to die for. In fact, a passion for God always involves risk, and it may involve doubt.

"If you have doubts, direct them to God," I encouraged the 240 teens. "You won't be telling Him anything He hasn't already heard. He wants us to come to Him with our doubts. After all, He's calling us to battle. He's calling us to an adventure. We are bound to have doubts. The Christian journey is not easy, and it's certainly not about being tame and nice."

The whole time I was presenting, a dark-haired, casually dressed boy, seated in the second row, waved his arm at me. I ignored him until I got to a place where I could break. I was a little surprised that he had interrupted my talk. I didn't recognize him but took the risk and asked, "Yes. Do you have a question?" I walked toward him.

"Yeah . . . well not really a question," he stood up as I approached, "but I just want to say, this is my third time here. My friend Ian invited me. I don't know much about God, but after hearing you describe being a Christian like a battle and a journey, that's what I want. I had a lot of doubts, but sitting here this morning I told God about them, like you said to do." He turned to the audience of his peers and boldly stated, "I am going to give my life to God today. I want to be passionate about following Him." He sat back down.

It couldn't have gone better if I had scripted the morning. "That's exactly what being passionate for God is all about. What's your name?"

"Tom."

"Tom, thanks for being bold and speaking up. It took a lot of courage to say what you just said. I appreciate you taking the risk to say it, and I appreciate your boldness and honesty to admit you need God. Let's thank God for Tom!"

Thunderous applause, whistles, and hoots.

I think Tom felt valued.

Discussion Questions

PARENT TO PARENT

1. Do you agree or disagree that today's children are susceptible to risks unknown to their parents? Explain your thinking.

2. What are some ways you can express that you value your teenager?

3. How do you respond to the statement, "The teens of the new millennium are isolated and unsupervised from adults"?

4. Did you receive a blessing from your parents? If yes, what

impact did it have on you? If not, what impact could a blessing have had?

5. When it comes to trying to understand youth violence, what indicators are there that our culture is suffering from sickness of the soul?

TALKING WITH YOUR TEEN

1. How does our culture put an emphasis on having the perfect body?

2. How can parents show they value their teens?

3. Does it take a village to raise a teenager? Why do you think that?

4. How can we do a better job of establishing community between generations?

5. Do teens need rites of passage? If so, what should they look like?

Responding to the Cry

THE CRY

The cry to be valued.

THE CHALLENGE

To make time to help our teens feel valued, particularly at key times of transition.

TOOLS TO USE AT HOME

1. Rent the video *Rudy* about a highly devoted but undersized college football player. Watch it with your teenager and

discuss the obstacles Rudy overcame to become a player. How did Rudy's personal sense of value help him?

2. Purchase two small mirrors, one for you and one for your teen. With a permanent Magic Marker or metallic paint pen, write the reference 1 Samuel 16:7 and the words *God looks at the heart* on the mirror. Place one where your teen will see it daily and the other where you will see it. Read the verse and discuss it with your teenager.

3. Do a Bible study with your teenager on who we are in Christ. Try to find as many verses as possible that describe who we are as a Christian. Write them down. When you have about a dozen or more, type them up on the computer, using a nice font and frame it. Examples: I am a child of God, 1 John 3:1; God's chosen people, Colossians 3:12.

4. To help you value your teens, maintain a file on them. Look for things like names of friends, favorite ice cream, favorite places to eat, video games your teen likes to play, favorite clothing brand and store, ideas for gifts, favorite snack. Allow the information to come up naturally. (Do not interrogate your teen!) Record the information. I use my personal digital assistant. When you have time, you can surprise them with a thoughtful gift. Paying attention is an effective way to demonstrate you value your teen.

5. Look at the rites of passage (page 180) and discuss with your teenager which ones she would like to celebrate. Start recording ideas for activities to incorporate into the celebration.

TOOLS TO USE AT CHURCH

To affirm the children and teens of your church, recruit a Barnabas Team of parent encouragers. Their mission is to plan rites of passage for the following occasions. Suggested gifts are also listed.

- Accepting Christ (youth Bible)

- Baptism (hand towel with Scripture reference stitched on it)

- Communion/Eucharist (pottery or pewter chalice engraved with the child's name)

- Preparing for adolescence (pocket knife or birthstone necklace)

- Purity pledge (a ring or cross necklace)

- Blessing (B.L.E.S.S. certificate and photo)

- High school graduation (memory book with photos, written advice from mentors, and blessing from parents)

For more information on planning rites of passage, see *Spiritual Milestones* by Jim and Janet Weidmann and Otis and Gail Ledbetter.

CHAPTER 7

A Cry for Support

The seventh cry of today's teens is the cry *to be supported in their efforts*. Our teens want us to support them in what is important to them. The concept of support seemed somewhat vague to me, so I asked a number of teens, "What does support mean to you? How would you like your parents to support you in your efforts?"

"I want them to be there when I need them."

"Support means feeling I am not alone with my problems."

"I think support would be giving me advice when I'm stuck or confused."

"Encouraging me when I am down or afraid."

"Support, for me, has to include motivating me. Sometimes I'm just too lazy to get going."

"Believing in me, having confidence that I can do it, and then letting me try—all the time being there as a safety net in case I blow it."

Eighty-seven percent of the teens surveyed in our Gallup "Cries of Teens" Survey reported that being supported in their efforts was a "very strong" need or "strong" need in their life.

What are they asking for?

Based on the survey, personal interviews, and my observations of millennials, I believe teens are asking for support through *connection, direction, and motivation,* and *letting go.*

You can see these themes in their comments.

✜ Be there when I need you (connection).

✜ Give me advice when I am stuck or confused (direction).

✜ Motivate me when I'm lazy (motivation).

✜ Give me more freedom (letting go).

The word *support* has its roots in two Latin words: *sub,* meaning under or close to, and *portare,* meaning to carry the weight. We get our English word *porter* from *portare.* A porter is a servant who carries the luggage or belongings of another. To support means to carry the weight or burden of another person. It conveys the ideas of physical contact and reinforcement, mental confidence and direction, and emotional encouragement and hope. The concept of support is biblical:

> Carry each other's burdens, and in this way you will
> fulfill the law of Christ.
>
> (Galatians 6:2 NIV)

We can be like Christ by carrying our teens' burdens. We communicate to our children that we will be there for them and that they do not have to carry the weight of their burdens alone. We can support our teens by sharing their loads.

I like what John Gottman writes: "The key to successful parenting is not found in complex theories, elaborate family rules, or convoluted formulas for behavior. It is based on your deepest feelings of love and affection for your child, and is demonstrated simply through empathy and understanding. Good parenting begins in your heart, and then continues on a moment-to-moment basis by engaging your children when feelings run high, when they are sad, angry, or scared. The heart of parenting is *being there* in a particular way when it really counts."[1] To connect with our teens, we need to be there for them, especially "when it counts."

Jesus demonstrated a keen sense of timing. He seemed to connect with people, particularly when they needed it. While adults were arguing rank and importance, Jesus embraced a child and rebuked them for being more concerned about competition than connection.

> He took a little child and had him stand among them. Taking him in his arms, he said to them, "Whoever welcomes one of these little children in my name welcomes me; and whoever welcomes me does not welcome me but the one who sent me." (Mark 9:36-37 NIV)

Jesus indicated His support for children by embracing them with affection, including them in the conversation, and by establishing that He values them. Children mattered to Jesus.

Likewise, our teens will feel supported by us when we connect, direct, and motivate them. How do we do that?

Support Is Learned

The most basic form of support can be seen when a parent instructs a child in an activity that is new to the child. In this interchange, we see connection, direction, motivation, and letting go.

Do you remember learning to ride a bicycle? I clearly remember my attempts to learn how to ride. I wonder why this was so important to me? Could it be that I needed my parents to be supportive of my efforts to learn how to ride a bike?

American teens, therefore, need to be called upon, not simply to live up to social norms—to fit in—but to be the helpers and healers that will begin to turn our society around. We need to look to teens to transcend culture, not simply to adapt to it. Teens learn support and teamwork at home. Most adults would guess that teen alienation has everything to do with peers, but it actually has more to do with what goes on in the home. The parents' level of support determines their teen's level of alienation. In the GYS we discovered that the alienated group reported a less-than-satisfactory home life. These teens have less opportunity to discuss their lives with the adults at home. They are less likely to see others reading at home and less likely to remember being read to. They wish they had more help with homework at home. They are also more likely to come from a household where food is scarce. The GYS also indicated that seven out of ten teens would like more time with their father. Six out of ten reported that they would like more time with their mother.

—*Gallup Youth Survey,* 24 October 1997, adapted

To be successful in teaching a child to ride a bike, a parent must connect with the child. I remember teaching our girls how to ride. I used the same method my father used with me. I removed one of the training wheels from my daughter's bike, after she'd ridden for months with it on. One Saturday I removed the other training wheel and instructed our daughter to hop on the seat.

"But Daddy, I'll tip over."

"You might, honey, but that's why I want you to learn how to ride your bike without training wheels. You have to get your balance to stay up on two wheels." I grabbed the handlebar and the seat to steady the wobbly two-wheeler.

Brooke perched herself precariously on the seat. "Now what?"

"Start pedaling, just like you would if you had the training wheels on."

"But I might fall; I can't."

"Just try it. I will be here to steady you."

"Okay, here goes." She slowly cranked the pedals; the bike began to move down the sidewalk. "Don't let go, Daddy!"

"I won't. I'm hanging on. Don't worry." I walked beside her with my left hand on the handlebar and my right on the back of her seat, maintaining the bike upright.

Her five-year-old legs began to push harder on the pedals, generating more speed. I began jogging to keep up with her. "Daddy, I'm doing it! I'm riding without training wheels!" She looked down at her legs, fiercely pedaling as the sidewalk became blurry.

Because she was looking down, she didn't see the light pole. I was still hanging onto the handlebars with my left hand, so I cranked them toward me. The bike swerved left and barely avoided the light pole. Surprised, she looked up. "What are you doing?"

"Steering. You have to watch where you're going. You have to be able to pedal and look ahead at the same time. You just can't look down at your pedals."

She raised her head and looked way down the sidewalk, "I can steer, Daddy. Let go."

I let go of the handlebars and ran alongside her for five paces, then shoved her forward with a big push. When I let go, I felt both worried and proud, worried that she might fall and hurt herself, proud that she was big enough and courageous enough to try it alone.

With a look of determination in her eyes, she took charge of her twenty-inch two-wheeler. The front wheel wobbled back and forth for fifteen feet, but she got control of it and guided her bike straight down the sidewalk.

"Way to go, Brooke! Good job! Keep pedaling. Don't stop or you will lose your balance. You're doing great. Keep it up!" I shouted as she pulled away from me.

She rode to the end of the block, down a driveway, and into the street. *What have I done? She's riding her bike in the street. Why did I teach her to ride a bike? She's going to leave me.* The thoughts crowded my head as I stopped to recover my breath.

Brooke whipped a turn and came back towards me. She stared down at her feet, which were pedaling furiously to keep her forward momentum. As she came closer, she looked up, and I saw a huge smile, "Daddy, look at me! I'm riding! Look! All by myself! *Wheee!*" She rode past me.

Our teens need us to support them. They need us to stay connected. "Don't let go, Daddy!"

They need us to direct and guide them. It's called *steering*.

They need us to believe in them and motivate them. "You're doing great! Keep it up!"

Support means connection, direction, motivation, and letting go.

Connection

Because God has designed us as relational creatures, we have an inherent need and drive to connect with other people and to belong to something bigger than ourselves. God created the family, in part, to meet this need, especially during our formative years. But as traditional families have increasingly come under attack, as more marriages dissolve and more "alternate family units" are formed, God's original design no longer exists in many households. The need hasn't gone away, however. We still crave and pursue meaningful relationships that fulfill the central desires of our souls for acceptance, affirmation, identity, and place. The sad truth is that if the home does not meet these needs, if the family no longer offers a place for kids to belong, they will find somewhere else to connect, either through peer groups or another organization.

Many teens are growing up alone. Sure, they may have a father and a mother, but they are abandoned emotionally. Many teens lead lives that are surrounded by other teens but devoid of any meaningful interaction with adults.

Many adults assume that today's teenagers want to be left alone. And because Mom and Dad are on their own search for significance and fulfillment, they isolate themselves from their kids. The result is that, more than in any previous generation, millennial teens lead lives that are without meaningful adult dialogue. Their parents may be there, but they're not connecting. Research suggests that most teens long for not just presence, but meaningful conversation.

Three-quarters of teens report that their parents usually know what is happening to them in school and that they often talk with adults about their interests or troubles. A majority (68 percent) also says that when they return from school, there usually is an adult at home. In blue-collar homes, teens are more likely to report an adult at home when they arrive from school. But this is less likely to be the case with older teens, white teens, and those living in suburban areas, perhaps because there is less concern about the safety of home for these groups.

BEING THERE

Jim Burns, noted youth speaker and youth worker, reports: "I have the privilege to speak and listen to thousands of young people each year. The number one request from kids for their parents is for a relationship with them. They seek their parent's time and attention. Please never underestimate the power of being there in your child's life. Two key points to remember are (1) bless your kids with your presence, and (2) bless your kids with affection."[2]

If 68 percent of teens have someone to come home to, why do so many feel alienated? Why do teens and their parents feel isolated from each other? Is it possible that being there is not enough? Is this generation unique, or do all teens feel estranged from their parents' generation?

In some ways, teens and parents from every generation feel a certain amount of distance between them. But with millenials it appears to be more extreme. If most of them come home to an adult, why isn't that making a difference? Could it be that having an adult *around* isn't the same as having someone to talk with?

Although their needs and cries are common, today's teens are likely to display their needs in a variety of ways. As a result, they are often alienated even in a roomful of peers. One teen cannot represent his school, let alone his generation. At one level, teens appear to have much in common, but if you look deeper you will find distinctive differences—in fashion, musical preference, values, and pastimes. These may seem small to the adult, but to teens, the distinctions are huge.

When I talk to adults about the millennial generation, I am often asked, "Are they ambitious or hostile? Violent or traditional?"

My response is, "Yes. Yes, this generation is all of those. It can be called the revival generation or the revenge generation. There are many who are ambitious and traditional when it comes to their values. They long for family and connection. There are others who are agitated and lashing out. They're a minority, but they're there."

BUSY AND LONELY

In a recent survey, one-fifth of teens surveyed scored high on alienation. They usually feel confused, pressured, ignored, angry, and lonely in school. They tend to think about death "often" or "almost always." These at-risk teens are also more likely to waste their time. They are more likely to hang out with friends after school rather than do homework. They like to cruise the mall or chill out at a friend's. They are not involved in after-school activities, but they find it difficult to get their homework done. Ironically, they spend a lot of time with their friends, and they still feel alienated.

Why is this? I believe that it's because teens are generally not equipped with the social skills they need to connect with another teen. They are lacking in social assets that strengthen relationships and work through conflict. As a result, they do not feel equipped to manage and maintain friendships. They feel alone.

Alienated teens report that life at home isn't acceptable. They report less dialogue with adults at home than other teens, they are less likely to have help with homework, and they are less likely to see their parents read. They are also more likely to come from households where food is scarce.[3]

Ideally, families provide opportunities to connect, create a sense of belonging, and provide for the needs of the children. When teens come home to empty cupboards and distracted parents, they do not feel supported. They do not feel like they belong or are connected with the family.

It seems that alienation may have more to do with what happens at home than with what happens at school. For years, we have believed the idea that teens face peer pressure and possible rejection, and that this can hurt their self-esteem and lead to alienation. But it appears that what happens at home is a huge factor in making teens feel alienated or accepted. Parents influence what happens in the home. By taking the initiative and making an environment where teens feels supported, parents are actually helping their teens connect with other teens.

CONSEQUENCES OF NOT CONNECTING

There is a cost to the lack of connection and support teens feel. They usually conclude that they do not belong. I know teens who admit to being confused, lonely, bored, or pressured at school. School becomes a negative environment for them, so they do not have motivation to do their homework. Instead they spend their afternoons with their friends. Many of these teens get wrapped up in death-oriented media to match their preoccupation with dying. They might be interested in dark musical groups. Teens in this group will sometimes alter their clothing to reflect their obsession with death and darkness. They do not feel like they fit in with the mainstream cliques at school, so they start their own. Some alienated teens begin high-risk behavior: substance abuse, sexual activity (often unprotected), going to after-hours clubs, learning to shoot guns and make bombs, visiting hate sites on the Internet, and ditching school.

Because they do not feel connected or supported, these alienated teens insulate themselves with cynicism and, at times, hate.

In survey after survey, many kids—even those on the honor roll—say they feel increasingly alone and alienated, unable to connect with their parents, teachers, and sometimes even classmates. They are desperate for guidance, and when they do not get what they need at home or in school, they cling to cliques or immerse themselves in a universe outside of their parents' reach—a world defined by computer games, TV, and movies where brutality is so common it is mundane. The parents of Eric Harris and Dylan Klebold have told friends they never dreamed their sons could kill. Theirs is an extreme case that has made a lot of parents wonder, *Do we really know our kids?*[4]

> There's a lot of anger in my generation. You can hear
> it in the music. Kids are angry for a lot of reasons, but
> mostly because parents aren't around.
> — Richard Rodriquez, 17[5]

Direction

A second necessary element for support is the guidance we offer our teens. Expressing "let's go in this direction" makes them feel supported and not lost in the juvenile jungle.

It's not enough to run alongside and steady the bike when your child is learning to ride it. Parents also have to help steer as their children are learning. Parents are more than buddies to their kids. They are to direct them to do what is right. Consider Abraham, one of the strongest father figures in the Bible.

> For I have chosen [Abraham], so that he will *direct his children* and his household after him to keep the way of the LORD by doing what is right and just, so that the LORD will bring about for Abraham what he has promised him. (Genesis 18:19 NIV, emphasis added)

Does your teenager believe you care about his choices and direction? Have you communicated to him that you are trying to direct him to "keep the way of the Lord," which is why you have rules that may seem unfair, though they are designed to help him know what is right and just? Connection helps us know our teens and make sure they know we understood them. Direction communicates, "Now that we understand each other, this is where you should go." Too many parents are passive and intimidated by their teens. They are afraid to go beyond connecting to directing. As a result, their teens do not feel supported. Parents are more than buddies with their kids; they are teachers.

> Fathers, do not exasperate your children; instead, bring them up in the training and instruction of the Lord. (Ephesians 6:4 NIV)

Ephesians 6 does not include anything about creating a multisensory environment that enhances a child's self-esteem. It's about training and instruction. It's about breaking bad habits and demonstrating how to develop good habits. It's about raising kids to know and follow the Lord. If we do direct our teens with training and instruction of the Lord, we are supporting them. If we do not, we are frustrating (exasperating) them.

The ultimate goal of Christian parenting is not to have kids who know about God. The goal is to have kids who have personal relationships with God and who believe God's Word is relevant for every aspect of their lives. It involves teaching our children the ways of God, helping them understand the character of God, and helping them to become sensitive to the darkness of their own hearts and the danger of walking alone and trusting in themselves. It involves teaching them the power of the cross and the provision of God's promises. God has called us to lead, guide, nurture, correct, and discipline our children, and He has sovereignly placed us in authority over our children. We must be willing to assume responsibility.[6]

Healthy families set limits, establish boundaries, and consistently enforce consequences. The parents are not afraid to train their children. This means correcting them when they do something wrong and directing them by instruction and example on how to do it right. Quality parenting is not easy, but it's worth it. Your job is to help your teen mature into a responsible young adult, not be their buddy.

Jim Burns, youth and family expert, aptly describes our role as parents:

> The purpose of parental discipline is to teach responsibility rather than to evoke obedience. There are many toxic ways to manipulate obedience, but if you use them, you will lose in the long run. Our goal as parent is to move from control to influence. As children move from dependence toward independence, a healthy parenting plan will move from extreme control toward influence. You can't be your child's best friend *and* be the person who enforces boundaries and limits. At each stage of development, your child needs something different from you when it comes to control, influence, and discipline, but what your child needs most is consistency.[7]

Our Family Core Values

honesty
We will communicate truthfully with each other.

honor
We will treat each other with dignity and respect.

truthfulness
We will uphold integrity in all we do.

righteousness
We will seek to be like Christ.

compassion
We will serve others, not ourselves.

diligence
We will work hard at what we do.

Our teens need consistent direction to feel supported by us. To help keep the end in mind, consider developing a map, a plan, to guide you along the way. By keeping the destination in focus and consistently referring to the map, you are more likely to get to where you want to be. Record in writing what is important to you. List these as your family core values. Discuss your family core values with your teenager. You may want to ask questions like these:

❖ Why do you think we chose these values?

❖ Which values have we emphasized most?

❖ Which ones haven't we emphasized much?

❖ What are some ways you have seen our family demonstrate some of these family core values?

❖ What suggestions can you make for developing some of these?

When we direct our teens with clear signals, they feel supported, which results in their increased confidence. Consistency by the parents leads to confidence in teens.

> Parents serve as important teachers, mentors, role models, playmates, companions and confidants.
> — U.S. Department of Health
> and Human Services

Motivation

The third necessary element for support is motivation. It's the keep-it-up-you-can-do-it form of support, the belief in your teenager that encourages him and gives him hope. Connection is physical—being there. Direction is mental—guiding to confidence. Motivation is emotional—giving courage to keep going.

I like to think of motivation as just the opposite of exasperation. (Remember Ephesians 6:4?) To motivate means to inspire and move toward action. To exasperate means to frustrate, block progress, and knock the spirit out of someone. Have you ever enthusiastically shared your excitement about a trip or a project with someone, only to have her say, "Oh, I hope you don't run into trouble in that country. I've heard terrible reports," or "That's a very ambitious project. It seems unmanageable. Are you biting off more than you can chew?" People who do this are *dream suckers*. They enjoy sucking the dream out of the heart of anyone who has passion, enthusiasm, or vision. They are dangerous people, and we are wise to avoid them.

Our teens need us to believe in them and their dreams. They need us to support them in their efforts to become responsible young adults. They need us to encourage—pour courage into—them and to lend them our hope when they feel hopeless.

I have loaned my hope to dozens of teens when they were ready to quit on life, their faith, their friends, their families. I say, "I know you feel you don't have any hope. Things look bad, and you expect them to get worse. But I want to loan you my hope. Would you like to borrow some of mine? I have a little extra right now, so I'll loan it to you to help you get through this tough time. But I'd like it back when you're finished with it. I may need it for myself later. No hurry though. Take your time."

I'm batting a thousand. Every time I have offered to loan my hope, the teen has looked at me with a smile and said, "Yes, I could use that." Each one of the following teens needed someone to believe for them what they could not see for themselves:

- Erin (15) was admitted into a psych unit for depression.

- Scott (17) doubted his faith and God's existence.

- Angela (16) starved herself into ICU with anorexia.

- Sheryl (18) was a suicidal victim of rape.

- Tom (13) was arrested for selling marijuana.

- Jeff (14) was addicted to Internet porn.

- Germaine (15) had sexual intercourse with his girlfriend.

- Allison (16) was grieving over her dad's death.

Every one of these kids made it through their dark valleys and returned my hope to me. I was then able to loan it to others. Most of them said something like, "I wouldn't have made it without your loan of hope. It gave me the extra nudge I needed to keep going."

I will never forget what Erin and Sheryl told me, six years and three hundred miles apart: "Your loaned hope kept me alive."

Our teens need adults who have been around for a while and can say, "You'll get through this." They need parents who have hope in them when they do not have hope in themselves. John White expresses it well:

> What do children need? And how well can parents meet their needs? Children need acceptance. They need praise and appreciation. They need to learn they can trust their parents not to deceive them or to break promises. They need consistency and fairness. They need to feel that their parents understand their fears, their desires, their feelings, their inexplicable impulses, their frustrations, and their inabilities. They need to know exactly where the limits are, what is permitted and what is prohibited. They need to know that home is a safe place, a place of refuge, and a place where they have no need to be afraid. They need warm approval when they do well, and firm correction when they do wrong. They need to learn a sense of proportion. They need to know that their parents are stronger than they are, able to weather the storms and dangers of the outer world and also able to stand up to their children's rages and unreasonable demands. They need to feel their parents like them and can take time to listen. They need perceptive responses to their growing need for independence.[8]

Support means encouraging our teens to keep pedaling when they are learning to ride their bikes . . . or careening through adolescence. It's shouting, "Keep it up! You can do it! Don't give up now. You're getting the hang of it!"

Support means connecting, directing, and motivating; it also means letting go.

Letting Go

Just like we eventually have to let go when we are training our children to ride bikes, we need to give them a shove and let them go as they grow to adulthood. We do not have an alternative. Can you imagine a parent running alongside her son's bicycle, steadying him as he rides to middle school? Sometimes support means letting go.

Letting go communicates to our teens that we believe in them. We are saying, "I've provided connection, direction, and motivation. Now I'm letting you go because you can take it from here." But letting go isn't always easy—particularly for the parent. We have thoughts like these:

- But I'm not finished with you yet!

- Are you sure you can handle this?

- What will you do if you fall or fail?

- Without you I feel lost.

These thoughts are normal. Don't worry.

Recently I had these feelings resurface. It had been sixteen years since I'd taught our oldest daughter to ride her bike, but I still had to apply the lessons I had learned then: connect, direct, motivate, let go.

As I drove Nicole to the train station, I felt that I should say something to her, something profound, something inspirational and wise, something fatherly. But all I could think of was, "Do you have enough money?" Then later, "Did you bring a water bottle?" Nothing else seemed to fit.

What do you say to your adult child who is going on a six-hour train ride to visit her boyfriend who is away at college? I had already presented my lectures on sex, dating, and choosing a mate. I even had written my thoughts in letters to her. It was time to shut up and let go. It was time to pray with her, kiss her good-bye and say, "I love you. I hope you have a fun time."

"Thanks, Dad. I love you too. Thanks for bringing me."

"Do you want me to wait with you or drop you off?"

"Just drop me off. I'll be fine."

As I pulled away from the train station, I glanced in the rear-view mirror and saw her standing on the platform, tall, secure, and excited. Meanwhile, I was feeling small, weak, and afraid. *What will happen to her? Will she be able to get on the train with all of her stuff? Will she have to sit next to a weirdo? Will she be okay?* I circled the parking lot one time to make sure she was okay. I wanted to park the car and sit with her until her train came, but she told me she would be okay. I wasn't sure, but I made myself let go. I forced myself out of the parking lot toward the freeway. I felt like I was abandoning her. I felt like I was letting her down. But I was letting her go, just like I did when I was training her to ride her bike.

Sometimes support means letting go.

CATCH AND RELEASE

I love the authenticity and vulnerability that Virelle Kidder shares in her book, *Loving, Launching, and Letting Go:* "We found the last few years of raising and releasing our children to be the most emotionally strenuous, perplexing, and faith-stretching of all. There seemed no end to the amount of wisdom we needed to launch kids into adulthood, as well as patience, financial genius, humor and sympathy. No nerves were left unstretched. Loving, launching, and letting go are not unlike labor and delivery; the biggest strain and life-giving efforts are often the grand finale."[9]

I can relate. My struggle at the train station had more to do with me than it had to do with Nicole. I wasn't sure I had prepared her for the challenge ahead. But for me, in that situation, the way to support her was letting go. It was not easy, but I tried to remind myself that we had spent time getting her ready for such a time as this.

FOUR WAYS TO KNOW IF TEENS ARE READY

Virelle Kidder offers a helpful checklist for letting go. There may not be a magic formula for ensuring success, but these are four fairly accurate ways to measure our teen's readiness to live on his own. Parents can aim at these areas of maturity as the countdown to launch progresses. These areas have nothing to do with outward appearances or academic achievement. Rather, they are indicators of character, wisdom, and spiritual maturity. As you look at the young adults in your own home, consider these four questions:

- Are they able to stand on their own two feet without your continual help?

- Do they demonstrate some degree of wisdom and maturity in their lifestyles and decision making?

- Can they maintain healthy relationships within the home and outside of it?

- Of chief importance to Christian parents, do they have an authentic walk with God that will impact every other relationship?[10]

GETTING TO KNOW YOUR TEEN

It's easier to let go of our young adult children if we know they are ready for it. If they are prepared and we trust them, we can let them go. But how do we know if they are ready?

Teens want to know and be known by their parents. The notion of the Generation Gap from the '60s—"just leave them alone"—does not apply to millennials. They want to connect. They want to be understood. They even want to know you! Millennials are crying out for more regular contact with adults who care about them and respect them. They want to contribute to the dialogue about things that concern

them: protection from drugs, violence, gangs; financial and environ-
mental issues; and how to build community in their world, which
seems so desperate for it.

> Are peers and the media the most powerful influ-
> encers of today's teenagers? Do they determine all val-
> ues and beliefs? According to researchers, the answer
> is no. Studies agree that parents remain the single
> most important influence, all the way through high
> school.
> — Wayne Rice and David Veerman[11]

According to the Gallup Youth Survey results, a majority of teens
report having at least one meal a day with their family, and most enjoy
it—encouraging news! Giving your teen a place to belong and be heard
may be as simple as a family dinner. Just make sure you turn off the
TV during the meal. Fifty percent of the teens surveyed reported that
they watched TV the last time they had a meal with their parents. They
also reported that a majority (56 percent) said grace or prayed prior to
eating the last time that they shared a meal with their parents. This figure rises to nine in ten of African American teenagers' households.
Most talked about school (66 percent) or family problems and interests
(53 percent), and most helped with the dishes afterward (65 percent).

A grandpa from rural Tennesee recently told me, "You want to
know what appliance will hurt the family?"

"Sure."

"Guess."

"The TV?"

"Nope. The dishwasher! When a family makes a meal together,
eats a meal together, and then washes dishes together, they learn to
serve each other and talk. They have to. What else they gonna do?"

Our findings indicate that some families are doing a good job of
connecting with their teens. Let's say we want to improve by attempt-

Gallup Youth Survey[12]

Teens were asked, "Which of these statements describe your family and your life at home?"

Statement	Percentage of Teens Saying Yes
Your parents usually know what is happening to you in school.	75
At home, you often talk with adults about things that interest you or are troubling you.	75
Your family usually eats at least one meal together each day.	71
You enjoy family mealtime.	69
You wish you could spend more time with your father.	68
When you go home from school, there is usually an adult there.	68
You wish you could spend more time with your mother.	64
On weekends your family does a lot of things together.	55

ing a regular family dinner with conversation. What should we talk about?

First of all, a few guidelines:

⚜ Be positive—make dinner something to look forward to.

⚜ Save discipline and correction for later private moments.

⚜ Consider the atmosphere. At least weekly, try to have a food theme and decorate the table accordingly. Taco night can be extra fun with a sombrero full of chips in the center of the table.

Table Talk

Most teens are tired of hearing us talk about the dangers of alcohol and drugs. Some of them say, "Enough already," about the topic of sex. What do teens want to talk about more often?

- Family finances

- Religion and faith

- School

That's right! Two topics most parents want to avoid—money and religion—are topics teens would like to talk about more.

I often ask parents to guess what topics teens would like to discuss more. I have asked this dozens of times to hundreds of parents. Not one has ever guessed family finances. Why do our teens want to talk about money? I believe it could be that they have heard that "today's teenagers are the first generation to grow up with less than their parents." They have also seen Mom and Dad go to work to make ends meet. Most teens can't figure out where all the money goes. (Of course, most think more should go to them!) I suggest going through the bills, the checkbook, and the monthly budget with your teenager. Let her see your financial priorities and some of the nonnegotiables (rent or mortgage, insurance, utilities). Be prepared to discuss the issues he or she is interested in. For more information check out *www.crown.org* and *www.mm4kids.org*.

Anything we can do to understand and support our teens increases the trust level and enhances the obedience level. Teens are more likely to obey when they feel we value our relationship with them. If we show respect for them, they are more likely to demonstrate respect for the rules we say are important. Become a student of your teenager. Use the chart on the next page as your guide.

Teen/Parent Topic of Conversation[13]

Teens were asked whether they would prefer to discuss the following topics with their parents more frequently, at the same level, or less frequently.

Topic	More	Same as now	Less
family finances	38%	35%	27%
drugs	33%	43%	24%
drinking	27%	44%	29%
religion	34%	42%	24%
school	33%	39%	28%
politics	31%	29%	40%
sex	20%	49%	31%

Here are some facts to help:

- Teenagers account for roughly 10 percent of the U.S. population.

- Half of teens have lived through their parents' divorce.

- Sixty-three percent come from homes where both parents work outside the home.

- There will be 35 million teens in 2010, a population bulge bigger than the baby boom at its peak.

- Teens are bigger, richer, better educated, and healthier than teens during any other time in U.S. history, yet many are at risk.

- The average teenager spends three and a half hours alone every day.

- Forty-seven percent of teens use the computer to go online. Most of them are e-mailing friends or checking out Web sites or doing research for school.

> ### How Well Do You Know Your Teenager?
>
> 1. Who is your teen's best friend?
> 2. What is your teen's favorite radio station?
> 3. Does your teen have a nickname at school? What is it?
> 4. Who is your teen's greatest hero?
> 5. What is your teen's most prized possession?
> 6. What is your teen's biggest worry?
> 7. What career is your teen considering?
> 8. What class at school does your teen like the most?
> 9. Who is an adult friend (outside your home) your teen has a good relationship with?
> 10. What does your teen like to do in his or her free time?

❖ Eight-five percent of teens say their mothers care "very much" about them. Fifty-eight percent said the same about their fathers.

❖ Teens spend 11 hours per week watching TV, 10 hours listening to music, 4.1 hours doing chores, 4 hours going to parties, and 2.5 hours at religious functions.

❖ One out of four teens considers suicide each year.

❖ Teens average just under $100 in total weekly spending.[14]

Maggie's World

Fourteen-year-old Maggie walks home from high school every day at 2:30. She has to get home before her ten-year-old brother and twelve-year-old sister. Maggie has the house key and the responsibility of watching her siblings, supervising their homework and finishing her own, cooking dinner, and picking up the mess before her mom and stepdad get home around 6:30 P.M.

"I wish my parents would make up their mind," she says. "One minute they treat me like an adult, with all this work I do for them, and the next, they treat me like a kid, especially on weekends. It's like they want a third parent on the weekdays, but I go back to being a child on the weekends. That's when I want to go out with my friends. Some days it gets lonely, and I wish my mom were around. Basically, I have a life of my own."

Teens often juggle as many roles as their folks, taking charge of housework and family meals, being involved in extracurricular activities at school, doing homework, and working long hours at a job. Since adults are often missing in action (keeping in touch with their kids through cell phones and pagers), friends nurture and counsel each other, creating their own community. Sure, a lot of parents balance the stress of their job and their parenting responsibilities by planning the time they spend with their kids—going out for family dinners or concerts or movies instead of watching TV. But there are many other parents who simply are not around, physically or emotionally.[15]

Teens Desire Our Support

In our Gallup "Cries of Teens" Survey, we discovered some interesting facts. Older girls (sixteen to seventeen) reported a much higher need to be supported than younger boys (thirteen to fifteen). Eight-one percent of these girls reported that the need to be supported in my efforts was a "very strong" need in their lives, contrasted to the boys group at 56 percent and the older boys group (sixteen to seventeen) at 68 percent. Girls, particularly older teens, keenly feel the need to be supported. It could be that boys are not aware that they need support yet. Culturally, males are not encouraged to seek support; they are encouraged to be the macho, lone cowboy.

Where they live influenced teens' responses. Rural teens reported the lowest response. Only 57 percent expressed that the need to be supported in their efforts was "very strong." Urban teens reported the highest need at 73 percent, followed by 65 percent of the suburban teens. It's likely that the rural teens feel supported because of stable, extended-family relationships. Growing up on the farm, often with Grandpa, Grandma, and Uncle Steve nearby, seems to make a difference for rural kids.

Regarding this cry, the most at-risk group is urban, African American females (sixteen to seventeen), who reported the highest need to be supported. I believe this is due to feelings of being vulnerable and unprotected.

Teens whose parent (or the chief wage-earner) is a blue-collar worker were also more likely to indicate support is very much a need in their lives (76 percent). Teens who have college-educated parents reported that support was a much lower need (58 percent). Teens feel more capable, valuable, self-sufficient, and supported when their parents have some college education.

Children Are Like Arrows

> Like arrows in the hands of a warrior are sons born in one's youth. Blessed is the man whose quiver is full of them. (Psalm 127:4-5 NIV)

Our children are like arrows. When they are young, we keep them safe in our quiver—the home.

As they mature, we pull them from the confines of the quiver and prepare to send them out. We *connect* with them by touch. They belong to us. We hold them in our hands. We *direct* them by pointing them in the right direction. We guide the arrowhead toward the target. We *motivate* them by adding pressure—pulling back on the bowstring. As we do, we are still connected and aiming. We check our aim, make sure we are still connected, pull further, and then release. We *let go.*

God has entrusted us with our teens—our arrows. He has blessed us with them. For some of you, this may be hard to recognize, so repeat after me, "God has blessed me by giving my teenager to me." Say it again.

Support means connecting, directing, motivating, and letting go. As in archery, if any one of these is missing from parenting, the results can be disastrous. Imagine an archer who does not hold the arrow carefully, or aim it with precision, or who haphazardly pulls back on the bowstring or does not want to release the arrow.

Ridiculous, isn't it?

Support your teen. Connect, direct, motivate, and let go.

Then you—and your teenager—will be blessed.

Discussion Questions

PARENT TO PARENT

1. Describe your experiences teaching your child to ride a bike.

2. How can we help our teens feel connected?

3. What do you think about the statement, "Most teens lead lives that are very adult-free"?

4. What do you think about family core values? Which are yours? What do you want to add?

5. What other word pictures beside riding bikes and shooting arrows come to mind when you think of supporting your teen?

TALKING WITH YOUR TEEN

1. Which element of support do you think teens need more of: connecting, directing, motivating, or letting go?

2. When do you feel like you and I connect? Disconnect?

3. Where could you use more guidance from me? Less?

4. How would you rate the topics of conversation found on page 213?

5. Do the exercise, How Well Do You Know Your Teenager? on page 214.

Responding to the Cry

THE CRY

The cry for support.

THE CHALLENGE

To take the initiative to support our teenagers by connecting, directing, and motivating.

TOOLS TO USE AT HOME

1. Once this week put down your paper, push back from your computer, and be as available-looking as possible when your teenager is home. Maintain your availability for sixty minutes. Sit on the couch, leaving a place for your teenager to join you. If your teen asks what you are doing, say, "Just thinking. You can join me if you want." See what happens.

2. Make an alienation poster with your teen. Clip photos and headlines from magazines and newspapers that represent things that may alienate teens. Discuss with your teen the reports that most school shooters felt alienated and persecuted. Ask if they know of anyone at school who appears to

be alienated. What could someone do to help? What could your teen do to help?

3. Schedule one-on-one time with your teenager every week. Consider the following ideas:

- eat breakfast at McDonald's before school

- go ice-skating or in-line skating

- attend a hockey game

- play basketball

- read a good book together

- visit a museum

- take art lessons

- go hiking

- play a board or card game

- play virtual reality video games

- ride bikes

- shop for cars

- design a family Web site

4. Some parents have found that their teens really open up when they tuck them in at bedtime—especially if they bring in milk and cookies. Take time at least once a week to tuck your teen in. If your teen feels too old for it, say, "I know you may feel too big for this, but let me do it for me." If he doesn't feel like talking, ask, "How about if I just pray for you?" Offer a short prayer that he will sleep well, have a good day at school in the morning, be safe, and live for God.

5. Design a family crest with your teenager. You can draw one or make it out of wood. Search the Web—check *family crest* or *heraldry*—to add some interesting possibilities to this activity. The symbols on crests represent virtues such as courage and perseverance.

TOOLS TO USE AT CHURCH

1. In your parents-of-teens group, assess how much time your teens spend alone. Guess how they spend their time from after school until bedtime in fifteen-minute blocks. Record your guesses, give the papers to your teens, and have your teens correct them. Compare your findings with other parents in your group. Discuss solutions for teens who have too much adult-free time.

2. Help the youth ministry team evaluate the ministry to see whether programs are being offered during the times teens are available. Some churches offer youth programs at times that conflict with sports and do not offer activities when students are bored or looking for something interesting to do.

3. Ask student leaders in the youth group for their input on designing ministries that might target alienated or bored teens. Brainstorm ideas and prioritize the top five. Ask, "What could we do with a little bit of money and a few adult volunteers that would make a huge impact on teens? What would really make them feel like they belong?" Try to make one idea a reality.

4. Ask a retail clothing store if you can borrow a mannequin for several weeks. Take the mannequin to a youth group meeting and announce, "Next week we are going to dress our mannequin with the best designer fashions. You are the

designers. Bring clothes and qualities you would like in an adult role model." The next week dress the mannequin with various clothes and virtues. Write the qualities and virtues on card stock, punch holes in the cards, string the cards with yarn, and hang them on the mannequin.

When finished, announce, "This is what you want in an adult role model." Read the elements. "We will station this in the church lobby because we need more leaders like this. In fact, three out of four teens feel that adult role models are missing from their lives. Our goal is to help you have someone like this—but hopefully living!"

5. To create a sense of belonging and connectedness in the church, invite several church members to the youth group to share their faith journeys and how they have made major decisions in their lives (college, career, mate, business, etc.). Make sure you provide time for questions at the end.

Responding to Teen Cries

We have read about the Seven Cries of today's teens. The response is up to us. Will we heed their cries? Will we reply to their requests for attention? Or will we get back to our routines, avoiding their cries with the busy hubbub of our schedules? You may be struggling with *if-onlys*.

- If only I had been a better parent.

- If only we hadn't gotten a divorce.

- If only we lived in a better neighborhood.

- If only I had more help.

- If only I had more money.

Parents of teens frequently ask me, "Where did I mess up? Am I missing something here?"

I remind them that God was the perfect parent. He created the perfect man and the perfect woman and placed them in the perfect environment. It was the best neighborhood around! And look what happened! Who are we to think that we can be parents and not have challenges with our teens too?

God understands what it is like to be a parent. He knows what it is like to have rebellious children. He knows the pain of losing children to death. He also knows the joys of new life and the prodigal who returns home. You are not alone in your parenting. God understands and is compassionate. He can relate.

Remember

When you are weary and ready to throw in the towel,
Remember, you are not alone.
When your teenager pushes all of your buttons and you are
    ready to explode,
Remember, you are not alone.
When your teenager comes home at 2:00 A.M. reeking of alcohol,
Remember, you are not alone.
When your teenager introduces you to her new boyfriend
    (who is 19 when she is 15),
Remember, you are not alone.
When your teen fails a test, gets cut from the team, doesn't get
    asked to prom, or breaks up with his girlfriend,
Remember, you are not alone.
When your teen loads all of her stuff into her Honda (including
    her favorite stuffed pig) and waves to you as she drives
    off to college,
Remember, you are not alone, even though you feel alone.
God is with you.

> Being confident of this, that he who began a good
> work in you will carry it on to completion until the
> day of Christ Jesus. (Philippians 1:6 NIV)

You are not alone. God is at work within you and your teen. He is committed to helping you complete the task of preparing your teen to be a mature, godly, young adult.

I know there is so much work to be done to get our teens ready for life. But here's the secret: *We don't have to do it all!* God will send people into our teens' lives to complete them. God will send some sandpaper, files, and rasps into their lives to finish off the rough edges. To put it into perspective, remember this: *God is more committed to completing the good work He began in your teen than you are.*

We do not have to do it all before our teens leave home. The finishing day is not when they move out; it's when Christ comes. That is why it may take more than the eighteen years you have with your child.

But what will you do with the time you have? How will you respond to the Seven Cries of today's teens?

Remember when your teen was a baby and cried in the middle of the night? Chances are, you got out of your warm, comfortable bed and responded to your child's cry. It would be insensitive to ignore your child's cries and not meet her needs. It would be ridiculous to hear your baby cry and go next door to tend the needs of the neighbor's child. You focus on the cries of *your* child.

The same is true for teenagers. We each need to heed the cry of our own teen and seek to meet his need. We do not need to respond to the cries of the kid next door. We do not need to respond to the cries of the teens at the middle school. We do not need to respond to the cries of every troubled teen we see loitering and smoking on the corner. *We respond to the cries of our own teens.*

Every parent needs to respond to the cry of his or her own teenager. If we all did, we would have an entirely different scenario with today's teens. But it takes getting out of our comfortable chair, bed, or routine to engage our teens. It takes commitment to provide security and refuge. Our teens will feel secure when we respond to their needs. And home will become a refuge from the adolescent storm.

There will never be an ideal time to build a relationship with your teen. There will never be an ideal time to teach. There will never be an ideal teen or an ideal parent to guide the maturing process. All you have is the reality of this day, this teen, and who you are.

In a country that has been rocked to its foundation, it is crucial that we provide security and refuge to our teenagers. Security is more than public safety; it's inner confidence: I'm trusted, loved, and have a purpose. It's the sense: I'm being heard and have value. These are ways we can support our teens in uncertain times.

These are gifts that only parents can give their children. If children fail to receive these gifts from their parents, they have difficulty acquiring them later. Everything depends on whether the modern American family can provide a secure refuge for our teens—a shelter.

A place where their cries are heard.

Appendix A

Conflict Pie

Divide the circle into pie-shaped wedges that reflect the greater and smaller areas of conflict in your parent/teen relationship. If you have many areas of conflict, you may want to focus on the main ones only. Label each piece of the pie according to the particular conflict it represents, and size it according to the intensity of that category's conflict. You can use the categories listed below or create your own.

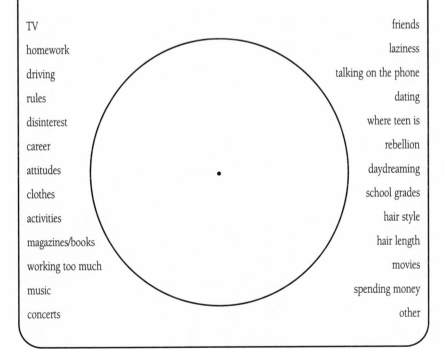

TV	friends
homework	laziness
driving	talking on the phone
rules	dating
disinterest	where teen is
career	rebellion
attitudes	daydreaming
clothes	school grades
activities	hair style
magazines/books	hair length
working too much	movies
music	spending money
concerts	other

Notes

Notes to Introduction

1. "Poll Shows Teens Try Hard, Enjoy Life," *Ventura County (Calif.) Star*, Sunday, 29 August 29 1999, D-9. Complete survey at *www.counton-shell.com/shellpoll.html.* Survey by Peter D. Hart Research Associates for Shell Oil Company.
2. Adapted from Wendy Murray Zoba, "Elegy for a Jesus Freak," *Christianity Today*, 6 December 1999, 88. Emphasis added.
3. Ibid.
4. William Strauss and Neil Howe, *The Fourth Turning: An American Prophecy* (New York: Broadway Books, 1997), 293.
5. Peter Zollo, quoted in Rick Lawrence, ed., *Trendwatch: Insights That Fuel Authentic Youth Ministry* (Loveland, Colo.: Group Publishing, 2000), 27.

Notes to Chapter 1

1. John Rosemond, *Teen-Proofing: A Revolutionary Approach to Fostering Responsible Decision Making in Your Teenager* (Kansas City: Andrews McMeel Publishing, 1998), xii.

2. Haim Ginott, *Between Parent and Teenager* (New York: Avon Books, 1982), 23.

3. Walt Mueller, *Understanding Today's Youth Culture* (Wheaton, Ill.: Tyndale House, 1994), 340.

4. Rosemond, *Teen-Proofing*, 15-16.

5. George Gallup Jr., and Alec Gallup, "Teens and Parents Getting Along Better," *Gallup Youth Survey*, 7 February 1996.

Notes to Chapter 2

1. This Gallup Youth Survey, conducted from December 2000 to February 2001, was based on telephone interviews with 501 persons aged 13 to 17 nationwide. It was conducted exclusively for this book.

2. John Trent, *Be There! Making Deep, Lasting Connections in a Disconnected World* (Colorado Springs: WaterBrook Press, 2000), 5.

3. Christopher John Farley, "Kids and Race," *Time*, 24 November 1997, 88.

4. *YouthViews: The Newsletter of the Gallup Youth Survey* 6, no. 8 (April 1999): 1.

5. For more information, visit *www.heritagebuilders.org.*

Notes to Chapter 3

1. George Gallup Jr., "What Americans Believe About Fatherhood and the Role of Religion," *The Faith Factor in Fatherhood: Renewing the Sacred Vocation of Fathering*, ed. Don E. Eberly (Lanham, Md.: Rowman & Littlefield), 39.

2. Michael McManus, cited in Gallup, "What Americans Believe About Fatherhood," 43.

3. Ibid., 44.

4. Ibid., 55.

5. Colin L. Powell, "Worry About the Children," *Ventura County (Calif.) Star*, 20 June 1999, D-9.

6. Adapted from Michael Medved and Diane Medved, *Saving Childhood: Protecting Our Children from the National Assault on Innocence* (New York: HarperPerennial, 1999), 205.

7. Nancy Gibbs, "Special Report," *Time*, 31 May 1999, 33.

8. Ann Oldenburg, "Parents See Violence, Not Sex, as Biggest Concern with Media," *USA Today*, 6 May 1999, D-1.

9. Reported in Adam Cohen, "Criminals as Copycats," *Time*, 31 May 1999, 38.

10. James Garbarino, *Lost Boys: Why Our Sons Turn Violent and How We Can Save Them* (New York: The Free Press, 1999), 5.

11. Michael Gurian, *A Fine Young Man* (New York: Jeremy P. Tarcher/ Putnam, 1999), 12-13.

12. Garbarino, *Lost Boys*, 15-16.

13. *Gallup Poll Releases,* 23 April 1999, 1.

14. *Gallup Poll Releases*, 21 May 1999, 1-2.

15. Ibid., 5.

16. Ibid.

17. Ibid., 4.

18. Ibid.

19. Medved and Medved, *Saving Childhood*, 221.

20. Adapted from "Teens Often Live in a Climate of Fear, Uncertainty and Danger," *Gallup Poll Releases*, 28 April 1999, 1-3.

Notes to Chapter 4

1. Charles Colson and Nancy Pearcey, *How Now Shall We Live?* (Wheaton, Ill.: Tyndale House Publishers, 1999), 139.

2. Francis A. Schaeffer, *He Is There and He Is Not Silent* (Carol Stream, Ill.: Tyndale House Publishers, 1972), 147.

3. Colson and Pearcey, *How Now Shall We Live?*, xi.

4. Ibid.

5. C. S. Lewis, *The Weight of Glory* (Grand Rapids, Mich.: Eerdmans Publishing, 1949), 86.

6. Adapted from Joe White and Jim Weidmann, general eds., *Parents' Guide to the Spiritual Mentoring of Teens: Building Your Child's Faith through the Adolescent Years* (Wheaton, Ill.: Tyndale House Publishers & Heritage Builders/Focus on the Family, 2001), 105.

7. William Strauss, interview, Fall 1996, quoted in Wendy Murray Zoba,

Generation 2K: What Parents & Others Need to Know about the Millennials (Downers Grove, Ill.: InterVarsity Press, 1999), 64.

8. Zoba, *Generation 2K*, 65.

9. James Dobson, *Bringing Up Boys: Practical Advice and Encouragement for Those Shaping the Next Generation of Men* (Wheaton, Ill.: Tyndale House Publishers, 2001), 250.

10. Colin L. Powell, "Worry About the Children," *Ventura County (Calif.) Star,* 20 June 1999, D-9.

11. *Gallup Youth Survey*, July 2000.

12. *Gallup Youth Survey*, December 2000–February 2001.

13. Adapted from Tim Smith, *Life Skills for Guys: Connecting Teens and Parents* (Colorado Springs: Cook Communications, 2000), 10-11.

14. Adapted from Tim Smith, *Almost Cool: You Can Figure Out How to Parent Your Teen* (Chicago: Moody Press, 1997), 162.

15. *YouthViews* 7, no. 5 (January 2000): 1, 3, citing a survey in the *Journal of the American Medical Association,* 10 September 1997.

16. "The Naked Truth," *Newsweek*, 8 May 2000, 58.

17. Princeton Survey Research Associates, reported in "A Snapshot of a Generation," *Newsweek*, 8 May 2000, 56.

18. D. Michael Lindsay, "A Generation on the Edge: Young People and Violence in the U.S." (report given at The George H. Gallup International Institute 2000 Ideas for Progress Seminar, Princeton, N.J., 15-17 June 2000).

19. George Barna, *Third Millennium Teens: Research on the Minds, Hearts and Souls of America's Teenagers* (Ventura, Calif.: The Barna Research Group, 1999), 24.

Notes to Chapter 5

1. *Gallup "Cries of Teens" Survey,* February 2001, unpublished.

2. H. Norman Wright and Gary J. Oliver, *Raising Kids to Love Jesus* (Ventura, Calif.: Regal Books, 1999), 64.

3. Albert Metowbian, *Silent Messages* (Belmont, Calif.: Wadsworth Publishing Co., 1971), 42-44.

4. Wright and Oliver, *Raising Kids to Love Jesus,* 74.

5. Adapted from "Entertaining Teens," *YouthViews* 7, no. 3 (November 1999): 4.

6. "Teens Go to Movies More Than Once a Month," *YouthViews* 7, no. 3 (February 2000): 3.

7. Ibid., 4.

8. Robert D. Putnam, *Bowling Alone: The Collapse and Revival of American Community* (New York: Simon & Schuster, 2000), 115.

9. Sharon Begley, "A World of Their Own," *Newsweek*, 8 May 2000, 54, citing William Strauss, *The Fourth Turning*.

10. Ibid., citing William Damon.

11. Patricia Hersch, *A Tribe Apart: A Journey into the Heart of American Adolescence* (New York: Ballantine Books, 1999), 54.

12. *Newsweek*, 8 May 2000, 54.

Notes to Chapter 6

1. *Webster's New World Dictionary*, 3d college ed., s.v. "worth."

2. John Eldredge, *Wild at Heart: Discovering The Secret of a Man's Soul* (Nashville: Thomas Nelson Publishers, 2001), 18. Emphasis added.

3. Patricia Hersch, *A Tribe Apart: A Journey into the Heart of American Adolescence* (New York: Ballantine Books, 1999), 12.

4. Ibid., 19.

5. Sharon Begley, "A World of Their Own," *Newsweek*, 8 May 2000, 55-56.

6. Hersch, 20.

7. Robert D. Putnam, *Bowling Alone: The Collapse and Revival of American Community* (New York: Simon & Schuster, 2000), 111-112.

8. Michael Medved and Diane Medved, *Saving Childhood: Protecting Our Children from the National Assault on Innocence* (New York: Harper-Perennial, 1999), 177.

9. Ibid., 178.

10. Hersch, 18.

11. Jim Weidmann, Janet Weidmann, J. Otis Ledbetter, and Gail Ledbetter, *Spiritual Milestones: A Guide to Celebrating Your Children's*

Spiritual Passages (Colorado Springs: Focus on the Family/Cook Communications, 2001), 81.

12. Pamela J. Erwin, *The Family Powered Church* (Loveland, Colo.: Group Publishing, 2000), 59.

13. Tim Smith and J. Otis Ledbetter, *Family Traditions: Practical, Intentional Ways to Strengthen Your Family Identity* (Colorado Springs: Focus on the Family/Heritage Builders/Cook Communications, 1998), 170.

14. Weidmann, Weidmann, Ledbetter, and Ledbetter, *Spiritual Milestones*, 41.

15. George H. Gallup Jr., "In Perspective: Views on the Gallup Youth Findings," *YouthViews* 7, no. 4 (December 1999), 5.

Notes to Chapter 7

1. John Gottman, *The Heart of Parenting* (New York: Simon & Schuster, 1997), 18, emphasis added.

2. Jim Burns, *How to Be a Happy, Healthy Family* (Nashville: Thomas Nelson Publishers, 2001), 6.

3. George Gallup and Alec Gallup, *Gallup Youth Survey*, 24 October 1997.

4. "Beyond Littleton: How Well Do You Know Your Kid?" *Newsweek*, 10 May 1999, 37-38.

5. Sharon Begley, "A World of Their Own," *Newsweek*, 8 May 2000, 55.

6. H. Norman Wright and Gary J. Oliver, *Raising Kids to Love Jesus* (Ventura, Calif.: Regal Books, 1999), 21.

7. Burns, *How to Be a Happy, Healthy Family*, 64.

8. John White, *Parents in Pain* (Downers Grove, Ill.: InterVarsity Press, 1979), 181.

9. Virelle Kidder, *Loving, Launching and Letting Go: Preparing Your Nearly Grown Children for Adulthood* (Nashville: Broadman & Holman Publishers, 1995), 15.

10. Ibid., 18-19.

11. Adapted from Wayne Rice and David Veerman, *Understanding Your Teenager* (Nashville: Word Publishing/Thomas Nelson, 1999), 117. Emphasis added.

12. *Gallup Youth Survey*, 22 August 1997.

13. *Gallup Youth Survey*, 10 July 1996.

14. Bret Begun, *Newsweek*, 10 May 1999, 38-39.

15. Patricia Hersch, "Home Alone," *Noise*, Summer 2000, 34.

Recommended Resources

Books

Barna, George, *Real Teens—A Contemporary Snapshot of Youth Culture*. Ventura, CA.: Regal Books, 2002. The section "Why teens are confusing to adults" is worth the price of the book; but there is so much more, especially the material on faith and spirituality.

Burns, Jim, *How to Be a Happy, Healthy Family*. Nashville, TN: Thomas Nelson Publishers, 2001. Discover ten principles to help your family succeed. Jim pulls from his years of experience as a youth pastor and father of teens to write a very useful and easy-to-read book.

Cloud, Dr. Henry and Dr. John Townsend, *Boundaries with Kids*. Grand Rapids, MI: Zondervan, 2001. Helping our children and teens take responsibility for their behavior, values, and lives.

Dobson, Dr. James, *Bringing Up Boys: Practical Advice and Encouragement for Those Shaping the Next Generation of Men*. Wheaton, Ill.: Tyndale House Publishers, 2001. A comprehensive, well-researched, and well-written book by a leading family expert.

Eldredge, John, *Wild at Heart: Discovering the Secret of a Man's Soul*. Nashville, TN: Thomas Nelson Publishers, 2001. A powerful, interesting quest into what makes a "real man."

Erwin, Pamela, J., *The Family Powered Church*. Loveland, Colo.: Group Publishing, 2000. A primer on how to value families in the local church.

Garbarino, James, *Lost Boys: Why Our Sons Turn Violent and How We Can Save Them*. New York: The Free Press, 1999. A call to make our culture more boy-friendly.

Gurian, Michael, *A Fine Young Man*. New York: Jeremy P. Tarcher/ Putnam, 1999. Outlines what it takes for a young man to mature and become a contributing citizen, sometimes against all odds.

Hersch, Patricia, *A Tribe Apart: A Journey into the Heart of American Adolescence*. New York: Ballantine Books, 1999. A popular and intriguing look at how our society has abandoned teens, then blamed them for it.

Kimmel, Tim, *Basic Training for a Few Good Men*. Nashville, TN. Thomas Nelson, 1997. A dummies' guide to becoming a godly man, baby-step by baby-step.

Lewis, Robert, *Raising a Modern-Day Knight: A Father's Role in Guiding His Son to Authentic Manhood*. Wheaton, IL: Tyndale House Publishers, 1997. I believe in the power of the message of this book and have incorporated it into how we train fathers.

Medved, Michael and Diane Medved, *Saving Childhood: Protecting Our Children from the National Assault on Innocence*. New York:

HarperPerennial, 1999. A provocative look at some of the common but toxic influences on our kids.

Mueller, Walt, *Understanding Today's Youth Culture*. Wheaton, IL: Tyndale House, 1994, 2000. This is an extremely well-researched compendium on how every aspect of youth culture is affecting your teenage child. I especially appreciate his work on the impact of music on today's teens.

Rice, Wayne and David Veerman, *Understanding Your Teenager*. Nashville, TN: Word Publishing/Thomas Nelson, 1999. Possibly the most useful tool for parents of teens because it offers advice for what you need the most.

Rosemond, John, *Teen-Proofing—A Revolutionary Approach to Fostering Responsible Decision Making in Your Teenager.* Kansas City, MO: Andrews McMeel Publishing, 1998. Refreshingly common-sense advice delivered in a humorous and practical fashion.

Smith, Tim and J. Otis Ledbetter, *Family Traditions: Practical, Intentional Ways to Strengthen Your Family Identity*. Colorado Springs: Focus on the Family/Heritage Builders, 1999. Dozens of ideas on how to use formal and informal times to strengthen your family.

St. Clair, Barry and Carol St. Clair, *Ignite the Fire: Kindling a Passion for Christ in Your Kids*. Colorado Springs: Cook, 1999. Barry is the expert on making young people disciples—starting at home. This is an excellent resource for a parents' book study or Bible study group.

Trent, John, Rick Osborne, and Kurt Bruner, *Parents' Guide to the Spiritual Growth of Children*. Wheaton, IL: Tyndale House, 2000. The instruction book that every Christian parent needs to get on the way home from the hospital with your baby. It is a practical, easy-to-use reference tool.

Trent, John, *Be There! Making Deep, Lasting Connections in a Disconnected World.* Colorado Springs: WaterBrook Press, 2000. In a culture that desperately desires to connect, this book shows how, beginning at home.

Weidmann, Jim, Janet Weidmann, J. Otis Ledbetter, and Gail Ledbetter, *Spiritual Milestones: A Guide to Celebrating Your Children's Spiritual Passages.* Colorado Springs: Focus on the Family/Cook Communications, 2001. Making the most of rites of passage with your child.

Wright, H. Norman and Gary J. Oliver, *Raising Kids to Love Jesus.* Ventura, Calif.: Regal Books, 1999. A comprehensive yet parent-friendly guide to help your child discover Jesus and grow spiritually through every stage of childhood.

Web Sites

Heritage Builders is a ministry designed to help build families of faith. Check out their free resources at *www.heritagebuilders.org*

John Trent's commitment to build strong families is well known. He has powerful and practical tools at *www.strongfamilies.com*

Jim Burns' ministry of building into youth workers and parents of teens has set the standard for integrity and effectiveness. Learn more at *www.youthbuilders.com*

Dr. James Dobson leads Focus on the Family—a ministry dedicated to the preservation of the home. Check out their many ministries at their Web site: *www.family.org*

Tim Kimmel's *Family Matters* ministry offers polls, resources, and conference information at his Web site: *www.timlive.com*

Integrity Publishers is continually producing quality Christian books; find out what's there for you at: *www.integritypublishers.com*